THE
SLACKER'S GUIDE
TO
LAW SCHOOL

SUCCESS WITHOUT STRESS

OTHER BOOKS FROM
THE FINE PRINT PRESS

ALSO FOR THE LAW STUDENT

Later-in-Life Lawyers: Tips for the Non-Traditional
Law Student

Law School: Getting In, Getting Good, Getting the Gold

Planet Law School II: What You Need to Know (*Before*
You Go)—but Didn't Know to Ask...and No One Else
Will Tell You

FOR THE SUMMER AND NEW ASSOCIATE

Jagged Rocks of Wisdom: Professional Advice for the New
Attorney

The Young Lawyer's Jungle Book: A Survival Guide

NON–LAW ADVENTURES

Grains of Golden Sand: Adventures in War-Torn Africa

Training Wheels for Student Leaders: A Junior Counseling
Program in Action

THE
SLACKER'S GUIDE
TO
LAW SCHOOL

SUCCESS WITHOUT STRESS

JUAN DORIA

THE FINE PRINT PRESS

HONOLULU

Copyright © 2008 by Juan Doria.

Published by:
The Fine Print Press, Ltd.
Honolulu, Hawaii
Website: www.fineprintpress.com
Email: info@fineprintpress.com

ISBN 13: 978-1-888960-52-5
ISBN 10: 1-888960-52-3
LCCN: 2008924773

Publisher's Cataloging-in-Publication Data:
Doria, Juan
        The Slacker's Guide to Law School: Success Without Stress
        Includes index.
        1. Law School   2. Legal Education
3. Law School—Practical Guides

Cover Design and Typesetting by Designwoerks, Wichita, Kansas.

The text face is Esprit Book, designed by Jovica Veljoviç and issued by ITC in 1985; supplemented with chapter headings in Castellar, designed by John Peters and issued by Monotype in 1957, and section headings in Poppl-Laudatio, designed in 1982 by Friedrich Poppl for the H. Berthold AG Typefoundry of Berlin.

Printed in the United States of America
15 14 13 12 11 10 09 08   10 9 8 7 6 5 4 3 2 1

CONTENTS

DEDICATION

To my beautiful wife. Without her encouragement, I would have never written this book. Without her support, I don't think I would have made it through law school.

ACKNOWLEDGEMENTS

While I have already dedicated this book to my wife, she should also be the first person I thank: for letting me read every section to her out loud, and for encouraging me to do the things I should do and dissuading me from doing the things I should not. I thank my daughter—though she cannot yet read—for being a welcome and positive distraction. Whenever she awoke from her naps and came to see me, I knew it was time to stop studying or writing.

To my cousin, who went to law school before me, and my brother, who went to law school after me, thank you for being my test audience. To my parents, for all their help, and to my sisters for not laughing when I mentioned I had written a book. To my grandfather, fine writer that he was, thank you for encouraging me to write.

To my professors and classmates, thank you for challenging me. And a special mention to my law school friends, thank you for all the help, the laughs, and the memories. We proved that there is plenty of fun to be had in law school.

The most important thank you goes to Thane Messinger, a man who knows books and knows the law. Thank you for keeping an open mind, taking a chance on this project, and for lending your vision, talent, and experience. Aloha.

FOREWORD

This was a harder foreword to write than those done for two other law books, *Jagged Rocks of Wisdom: Professional Advice for the New Attorney* and *Later-in-Life Lawyers: Tips for the Non-Traditional Law Student*. Coincidentally, as a result of this book yet another book for law students, *Law School: Getting In, Getting Good, Getting the Gold*, is being written. These books are not "competitors" (in the sense that we think of a *You-Win-I-Lose* competition) as much as they are different views of the same legal puzzle.

To be honest, I hesitated writing a review for this book—but not because of the concern above. Rather, I worried that some would read this book (if they get beyond its title) and assume that it appeals to our lazier side—or, worse, is seen as promoting a lackadaisical attitude toward the law in general or the study of law in particular.

To be even more honest, when I first read this book I was a bit put off. Here was someone who seemed to take advantage of hedonistic opportunities—vacations, weekends, parties—and who seemed not to be genuinely committed to the study of the law, or indeed to the law at all. I put the manuscript aside and, in fairness, gave it a second reading some time later. While I had the same initial reaction, as I went further into the book I saw a different picture emerge: one of an individual who had a sense of self, who was as decent as many of the friends I had known were, and who refused to be sucked in to the madness that overtakes many in law school.

While there can be a difference of opinion about who's "right" in their approach to law school, the deeper point is one that, I think, should be made. And it's one that Juan makes well: it is possible to survive, and even succeed, without succumbing to the darker forces that pervade the law school experience for many if not most students. It is important to qualify this with the note, however, that the competition you will face in law school is more fierce than you have ever faced before. Thus, if you're hoping to read this book and cruise through law school, you are likely to be sorely disappointed in the outcome. It *is* possible to cruise through law school and survive (although I hope that's not your goal); it is not possible to cruise and succeed. That written, much of what goes on in law school is irrelevant to winning or losing. It is thus easy to fall into a trap of assuming that one either strives and succeeds or slacks and fails. Those are false dichotomies, and this book speaks to this important point.

I encourage you to read what Juan writes, whether or not that is your approach, with an eye toward what can be absorbed to make *your* experience in law school better. Importantly, enjoying law school is not (or should not be) the opposite of learning the law. It is possible to do both, and much of the advice here will help in setting the right balance.

I thus recommend this book as it sits astride a spectrum of law books that range from this one to *Planet Law School,* which in its own right is perhaps the most comprehensive, if intense, guide available. Each of these books has much to offer its readers, and for that reason alone it's worthwhile to at least scan what each suggests. This is not about confusion or about overload, but rather about building an approach that works, and works *well,* for you.

*　　*　　*

My experience with the law (and within law school) was quite different than it was for Juan. There are, however, a number of parallels—and more than a few times in the second reading I laughed out loud over his descriptions of various tempests in the law school teapot. I too did not go to law school with the intent to practice law. I went to law school assuming and hoping that it would...*finally*...be the intellectual challenge I assumed higher education should be. As anyone who's been through law school will attest, this vision was at least partially misplaced. Law school quickly became a highly competitive, even hostile experience. This affected even the top of the class. In 1989, when I entered law school, unbeknownst to us a perfect storm was gathering: applications had hit all-time highs—leading to an even more exceedingly intense competition for a then-smaller number of seats—while the market for new attorneys was set to collapse in the recession of 1991. (This cycle followed a boom in the late 1980s, which in turn had followed a bust before that.) The legal job market is fickle, and with that the pressure on law students can intensify beyond even the insanely high law school norm.

In 1989-1991, the vocational impact invaded the halls. What seemed to be an ordinary level of stress mushroomed into a near-constant panic about jobs, jobs, jobs. As lists of law firms interviewing dwindled, desperation set in among nearly all. It is difficult for someone not of the law school world to accept, but under even normal circumstances the importance of one's standing in first year is important. In such a world as was faced in the early 1990s, it became consuming. There is simply no easy way to sufficiently convey the difference a few places in rankings means, either among or within law schools. This cannot help but infect everyone—or nearly everyone—in that world.

The importance of this book is in providing an antidote. Yes, the money (both the debt and hoped-for salary) are still important, but they will be important regardless of how you achieve your goal. The issue, then, is in accomplishing that goal—and in doing so without killing yourself and becoming a bad person (and bad lawyer) in the process.

Worse, there's a tendency to follow a herd mentality: the assumption that there's just one right way to do something, or just one way to study the law. Too often, this involves too much make-work, too much stress, and too much selfishness. Even that aside, as the saying goes there are different spokes for different folks, and so too are there different ways to do well in law school. Sometimes, it's important to pose a clear alternative—so that the right answer is achieved, whether or not it is *that* alternative. This book poses just such an alternative that might not have made its way to you otherwise.

* * *

I was surprised, by the way, when I saw the title for this book—the irreverent *Slacker's Guide*—and wasn't sure whether I should admire or dislike it. On the one hand, "slacker" certainly carries a negative connotation, particularly among those who populate law schools (and law firms). Much as we old fuddy-duddies should make fun of ourselves for being, well, old fuddy-duddies, there's a real risk in embracing the term and concept of a "slacker." The study of law is not easy, and anyone who takes a casual approach is almost certain to face soul-crushing disappointment, even and perhaps especially for the best of students.

On the other hand, much of what Juan speaks to is quite relevant, and is shared by, yes, us old fuddy-duddies. In particular, the negative environment that can develop in law school and the hyper-competitive assumptions that take root—which are, believe it or not, *against* what will be necessary and helpful in one's career—these are troubling to us all, and the essence of what is advocated here is, on the whole, a good and healthy approach.

I suspect that most readers will pick this book up to learn just what on Earth would be in a book with a title such as this one. *Slacker* certainly doesn't ordinarily go with *law school.* We might thus take the title as a good-natured, tongue-firmly-in-cheek poke at all of us. We attorneys can take ourselves a little too seriously, and it's important to know when (and how) to laugh. Law school can take even this sense of gravity to an extreme—as so much is riding on the outcome—that "too serious" can border on mental instability. In that sense, the title is just right. It's an antidote to this as well: to what can set in among law school and its inhabitants.

Even if you don't care for the title, or approach, if you pick up just a few good tips from this (or any) book, it will have been worth your time. That might be one of the lessons of how to do well without going crazy: picking up what you need to know, without making a huge fuss of it. If it doesn't apply to you, or appeal to you, then skip it and forget about it. In the grand scheme, there's no harm done, there might be a few lessons learned, and you'll find the approach that is right for you.

Other books, such as *Later-in-Life Lawyers,* speak to issues of special concern to those who enter law school later and with different and often greater constraints. If such applies to you, you might pick up a copy—at the library if not bookstore. A second book, as mentioned, is *Planet Law School,* which arguably sits at the opposite extreme from this book's approach. A careful reading of both books, however, will lead to a different conclusion. While the author of this book was ambivalent about his desire to practice law, and while the author of *Planet Law School* is passionate for the practice of law, both address the same essential questions, and arrive at much the same answer. Law school is not—or should not be— what many make of it. It should not be hyper-competitive, negative, caustic—even if that's what a forced curve and extraordinarily smart, Type-A personalities help to make it. Once you've graduated, you'll be *working* with these classmates…who will then go by the name colleague. If you've burned too many bridges, buying into the most negative elements of law school, chances are you will not have a happy experience in law practice, either.

Two other books I might recommend as long as I'm on a frolic, these relating to your first job as a summer or first-year associate, or for work during your second or third years of law school. First is *Jagged Rocks of Wisdom, Professional Advice for the New Attorney,* by Morten Lund, and the second is *The Young Lawyer's Jungle Book: A Survival Guide,* which I wrote out of my early experiences in practice. I hope the latter reference is not too self-serving, yet the import of both is consistent for all law students: learning the law is one thing; surviving in a law office environment is a different animal entirely. Both books suggest a careful, not uncontrolled, approach in navigating the dangerous waters of early law practice. While quite different, each in its own way shows you where the shoals are—and how to reach the safety of your own legal harbor.

Perhaps the great accomplishment of this book is that it takes a different…a refreshingly different…look at law school. Whether the approach in this book is for you or not, you will be better for having read it. If you take even a handful of helpful suggestions— and they are here—your time will have been well spent. Thus, an appreciation is due to Juan for his experiences and unique approach, and for taking the time to write about both.

In *your* journey, I wish you the very best.

Thane J. Messinger
Law School: Getting In, Getting Good, Getting the Gold
The Young Lawyer's Jungle Book: A Survival Guide
April 2008

INTRODUCTION

One possible evolutionary reason why human pregnancies are so long—nine whole months—is so parents will have enough time to come up with a proper name for their baby. Still, it seems that some parents botch even this basic responsibility, and their hapless child is the one to suffer for it. Likewise, perhaps the hardest part of writing a book is coming up with the title. Thousands of sentences are read and quickly forgotten, but the title sits there and stares at you, making eye contact that seems to follow you across the room.

This book is titled *The Slacker's Guide to Law School: Success Without Stress.* Whether the title is good or bad is for others (including you) to decide, but either way, it requires some explanation. First of all, it is a bit of a misnomer, since no law student can truly be a slacker, and no slacker can truly be a law student. Law school is tough work, and actual slackers don't tend to volunteer for three years of tough work. This is comparable to a cookbook titled *The Anorexic's Guide to Gourmet Cuisine.*

So this book is not exactly geared toward slackers who are pondering the idea of going to law school. Rather, it is intended for anyone attending, applying to, or considering law school. To this large group, it offers advice in the form of the "slacker approach." Though there is no escaping the fact that law school is tough work, most students make it tougher than it actually has to be. They study, work, and worry more than they really have to. This book and its slacker approach shows you that it is possible to cut the work in half, study efficiently, and get good grades, while keeping a level head and maintaining an enjoyable, relatively stress-free lifestyle. This approach is not for everyone, but just about anyone can benefit from it.

The second way in which the title might seem ill-conceived is that it promises the reader success. Success is problematic in that it is difficult to measure in many contexts, but there seems to be a general consensus on what constitutes success in law school. Essentially, you have to get into one of the top ten schools, graduate in the top ten percent of your class, and get a job as an associate in a top ten firm. I've met law students from all over the country, and only a *very* elite few meet this standard of success. Does this mean that all the *other* law students in the country are *not* successful?

Success should be determined by oneself. I'm not talking about rationalizing your shortcomings, but rather, knowing what is important to you, and setting your own goals to accomplish that. One of my goals is to achieve a healthy balance in life, where I allot adequate amounts of time to my professional, personal, and family lives. I like to get home at a reasonable hour and play with my daughter. Therefore, a job working 70-hour-weeks at a big law firm never seemed like a successful fate to me.

Coming into law school, at least during the first weeks, everyone seems to have noble goals and reasons for being there. If you ask others why they are in law school, or what they hope to do with their law degrees, you'll hear things like: "I want to help exonerate wrongfully convicted death row inmates" or "I want to help rewrite environmental protection legislature." The goals won't necessarily be noble. The most memorable answer I ever heard to such a question was from a friend whose heightened libido had a tendency to cloud his sense of legal ethics. When I asked him what kind of law he wanted to practice, he told me, "I want to be a divorce attorney, so I can sleep with my clients after I represent them." (Well, at least he added the "after" part.) But no matter how passionate these students are about their goals, an institutional notion of success begins to trump all. Eventually, nearly everyone goes for the big law firm jobs—or wants to. The ones who *get* those jobs feel successful, and the ones who don't feel like failures.

My advice is to define your own notion of success. The clearer this notion is in your head, the easier it will be to achieve your goals and the more satisfying law school will be for you. My friend achieved his goal of becoming a divorce attorney—though I don't suppose he seduces his clients as he is now happily married and has not yet been disbarred. Still, in one sense his motivation, while a bit twisted, was helpful to get him to where he is now: a satisfied attorney who has achieved the goals he set for himself. (Minus, of course, the sex-with-clients part, which he fortunately outgrew.)

The ability to define for yourself what you want—and then to actually achieve it—that's what I mean by success.

The final part of the title is the promise of achieving the aforementioned success *without stress*. Good luck with that. If you make it through law school without feeling *any* stress, you're either the Dalai Lama or you're comatose. There will be stress, but it is essential that you try to minimize it. Otherwise, it will hurt your performance. One of the few gifts I have been blessed with is the ability to remain unstressed during stressful situations. When I was a young basketball player, my coaches would be in awe of my ability to remain calm under pressure situations. Not to say that I was a great clutch player, or a great player at all for that matter. I just wasn't affected—negatively or positively—by the mounting tension of the game. My calm demeanor would sometimes be confused with stupidity, and others would suppose that I had no idea that our team was down by a point and there were ten seconds left. Sometimes I would be substituted for a more nervous player on the bench, or someone else would be asked to take the final panicked shot.

My approach to law school was very much the same. I simply did not let the stress get to me. Not when I was on call, not before exams, not during the job hunt. This drove some of my classmates crazy, and some of them even hated me for it. But instead of hating, they should have tried to mimic my approach. Anyone can do it, and it doesn't take hours of meditation. It just takes a conscious effort to remain calm when everyone around you is hysterical, and the consideration of some other tips included in this book. The slacker approach is not foolproof. There were times in law school when even I couldn't help but start to freak out. But you will be amazed by how much a lower level of stress will boost your academic performance.

So, now that we're clear on the title and the concept of the book, I'll leave you to read the rest (which is, I hope, self-explanatory) in peace. Enjoy.

THE
SLACKER'S GUIDE
TO
LAW SCHOOL

SUCCESS WITHOUT STRESS

1

SHOULD YOU GO TO LAW SCHOOL?

When I decided to go to law school, it wasn't because I necessarily wanted to become a lawyer. I wasn't particularly interested in the law. Instead, I decided to go to law school because I thought it was the perfect excuse to live by the beach for a few years and not have to work.

After college, I spent four months in Italy, traveling and partying under the guise of being an Italian language student. I was having the time of my life until I ran out of money and had to return to my dreaded hometown of Indianapolis, in the landlocked state of Indiana. My last month in Italy was spent on the beautiful island of Sicily, in a little tourist haven of a town called Taormina. I established a routine of spending days at the beach and nights at the bars, and although I was scheduled to return to the United States at the end of May, my real desire was to spend the summer, if not the rest of my life, in Taormina.

The obstacle was a lack of funds. Being a popular tourist town, Taormina is quite expensive, particularly during the summer, so I decided to get a job. I thought the perfect place to work would be the night club I frequented, *Café Mediterraneo*. I asked the owner, Tanino, if he needed additional help and he hired me on the spot, since English-speaking waiters were in high demand for the summer.

I showed up ready to work on a Wednesday night and worked my ass off from seven in the evening until about five in the morning. I took orders, delivered food and drinks, and tried to get by with my limited Italian. At the end of the night, Tanino thanked me, congratulated me on doing a good job on my first night, and handed me a single bill of cash. I thought it would be rude to survey the bill in his presence, so I put it in my pocket, thanked him, and said goodbye.

As I turned the corner on my way home, I took the bill out of my pocket hoping it would be a one-hundred *euro* note, or at least a fifty. It's not customary to tip waiters in Italy, so this single bill was my entire income for the night. As I unfolded it, I nearly vomited. He had paid me twenty *euros* for ten hours of work. Regardless of the current value of the euro, this was at the time when the euro was first introduced, and it was worth less than the American dollar. I had just forfeited a night of bar hopping with my friends to work for about $1.50 an hour. My initial thoughts are unprintable, while my later thoughts bring to mind the Ugly American: "If these Europeans think I'm going to serve them for anything less than the federal minimum wage of the United States (which at the time was around $5 an hour), they've grossly underestimated me."

I was scheduled to work again the next day so I reported for duty, but I told Tanino it would be my last night. He was upset since he was counting on me to work through the summer, but I could tell he wasn't surprised. He knew he couldn't afford any Americans on his staff. He paid me a bit more the second night, but it still wasn't nearly enough—especially when you consider the fact that a Sicilian Mafioso threatened to kill me.

This, of course, necessitates the telling of the tale: A confident-looking, bald-headed man, smoking a cigarette through a long cigarette-holder, finished eating, stood up, and simply began to walk out. Being loyal to my boss—and having no idea who the customer was—I stood in his way and told him he couldn't leave until he paid. He smiled at me and told me, "I don't pay." In my broken Italian, I responded, "Then you don't leave." Sicily has come a long way since its big mafia days, but still, certain Sicilians only pay their tabs if they feel like it, and no American kid with a *Eurail* pass is going to change that. Tanino was standing behind the bar, and the guy looked over at him as if to say, "Who the hell is this kid, and doesn't he know how dangerous it is to stand in my way like this?" I looked over to Tanino, and he gave me a look that explained it all. He violently shook his head and signaled toward the door. Then he took his thumb and slid it down his cheek, from ear to chin. I had been in Sicily long enough to know that this was the hand signal used to identify members of the mafia.

I liked Taormina so much that a part of me considered swallowing my pride and trying to make do with the miserable pay. But my encounter with the mafia put me over the top. I was an American with a college degree. Maybe I could handle the low pay under normal circumstances, but once fending off *mafiosi* became part of the job description, I required a raise, and maybe even some benefits.

I left Italy with a sad heart, fond memories, and absolutely no idea what to do next. After a few days in Indianapolis, I missed the beaches of Sicily too much, so I drove with a friend to Myrtle Beach, South Carolina for a quick fix of sand, ocean, and beach-town nightlife. It wasn't Taormina, but when you live in Indiana, you can't be too picky.

After a fun week in Myrtle Beach, on the long drive home, as my friend and I sat in complete silence, I thought about what to do next with my life. I figured the first step would have to be to get the hell out of Indiana. There was nothing there for me except a place to stay at my parents' house. I had to move somewhere where I could be happy, like I had been in Italy. However, to move somewhere, I needed a reason to go there.

I came up with a destination before thinking of a reason for going there. I thought about the things that made me happy. I had always liked the beach, but I had never had the fortune of living near the coast. I thought to myself, "Where could I go to be surrounded by the ocean and beautiful white-sand beaches?" The answer seemed obvious: Hawaii.

I pictured myself living in Hawaii, wearing shorts and flip-flops year round, hanging out at the beach all day, surfing, and drinking tropical cocktails. I got so excited over the idea of living in Hawaii, that if my friend's eyes hadn't been glued to the highway ahead of him, he would've asked me what the hell I was smiling at.

I had my destination, now I just needed a reason to actually go to Hawaii. I could put my bachelor's degree to work and try to find a job there. But if I were to work in Honolulu Monday through Friday, nine to five, that would hardly leave me any time to go to the beach or stay out late at night, other than on the weekends.

I thought back to my college experience at Indiana University. I loved college. A flexible schedule with only two or three classes a day, Fridays off, a little bit of studying here and there, a lot of partying, some intellectual stimulation, and a free gym. If I could have all this with Hawaiian landscapes in the background, I would be in heaven. I needed to go back to school, but what could I study?

I was an English major in college, but a Master's degree in English would be about as marketable as a certified lifeguard's license. I thought about an MBA, but they usually require a few years of work experience prior to enrollment, which I didn't have. I had always heard that a high percentage of English majors went on to law school. This had actually been the selling point when I tried to explain to my parents that majoring in English wasn't a complete waste of their money. Everyone thinks highly of law school, and my old-fashioned, professional-minded family would probably give more merit to a law degree from the University of Hawaii than to a Ph.D. in English from Harvard.

When I graduated from college, my grandfather, who is a retired engineer, called to congratulate me. Immediately after telling me congratulations, he asked me: "So when are you going back to school to get a *real* degree?" I thought the pursuit of a law degree would not only be the perfect excuse to spend three years in Hawaii, it would also get my concerned relatives off my back for a while.

As soon as I arrived home from the long drive from South Carolina, I ran upstairs, logged on to the internet, and accessed the University of Hawaii's website. After a few mouse clicks, my prayers were answered. *Eureka!* There actually *is* an accredited law school in the great State of Hawaii.

That night at the dinner table I announced to my parents that I had decided what to do with my life. They became silent and got a nervous look on their faces, like they were waiting for a doctor to announce the results of a diagnosis. I sat up straight and told them: "I've decided to go to law school..." My father, who is a doctor, smiled proudly, and my mother was delighted. They looked so happy and relieved, I hated to have to finish my sentence. I continued, "...in Hawaii." Their smiles vanished.

REASONS FOR GOING TO LAW SCHOOL

In retrospect, a desire to live in Hawaii is not the best reason to go to law school. Living in Hawaii still seems like a great idea, but using law school as a cover for a three-year Hawaiian vacation is pretty dumb. Of course, I only realize that now after graduating from law school (and having never made it to Hawaii).

There is only one good reason to go to law school: to become a lawyer. A law degree is a prerequisite for anyone wanting to work as an attorney, so if that's what you want to do, you should— actually, must—go to law school. But, if you're not absolutely, positively *sure* you want to be a lawyer, don't go to law school. Do something, anything, else.

Saying that you should only go to law school if you aspire to become a lawyer may seem like an obvious starting point, a throw-away piece of advice, but you would be surprised how many people go to law school with ulterior motives. In the past few years, people have been applying and enrolling in law school in record numbers, and new law schools—accredited or not—have been popping up all over the country to get a piece of the action. What's curious about this academic Gold Rush is that the few golden nuggets that every-one seeks...aren't all that desirable once found. Studies repeatedly show that lawyers are among the nation's least-satisfied profession-als. Lawyers rank low in job-satisfaction surveys, and high in cate-gories such as job-related stress, depression, and alcoholism. Sure, a "lucky" few enjoy high salaries, but who wants to get paid to work a job they hate and be driven to alcoholism by excessive stress? Apparently, a lot of people do, since so many eager students are lin-ing up at the doors in this country's various law schools.

Many decide to go to law school without really knowing what a lawyer actually does. All the John Grisham books-turned-into-movies and all the courtroom dramas on television make it seem as if an attorney's work is comparable to that of a superhero's. Many have the impression that once they become a lawyer they'll reenact on a regular basis the final trial scene in *A Few Good Men*. The truth is that only a modest fraction of working attorneys ever see a courtroom, and the few who do don't usually tackle cases as exciting as the ones seen in the movies. Understandably, screenwriters and producers omit scenes that might fail to entertain—and the real job of an attorney is, for the most part, deadly dull. Therefore, while a moviegoer sees Tom Cruise pound his fist on a table and yell at Jack Nicholson, we don't see him fumble through dozens of statutes and hundreds of case decisions, completing the necessary legal research, and building the case he is provided seamlessly by the fiction writers. If seen in real time—quite unlike reality shows—such real-world scenes would make for atrociously bad television.

Before you commit your life to the legal profession, do yourself a favor and find out what lawyers actually do. Talk to attorneys and ask if you can trail them at work. Get a job in a law office. Can you envision yourself doing what they're doing every day for the rest of your life? If, after serious thought and observation, the work seems interesting, then you might well want to go to law school and be on your way to a career in the law. If, however, you find the work to be mind-numbingly dull, run for your life. Forget about law school and find a different career path. Now is the time to find out, before you make such a serious commitment. Otherwise, somewhere along the line, you might realize that you're not all that interested in the law, and a career as an attorney will make your life miserable. By this point, however, you'll have dedicated so much time and money you'll feel that you have no choice but to continue.

The number of students enrolling in law school seems to increase every year. Like me, many of these up-and-coming stars are choosing to go to law school for all the wrong reasons. Following a most-unscientific poll, here are some popular reasons why many choose to go to law school:

I don't know what else to do. Anyone who has ever worked in an office knows about the art of looking busy. Before I went to law school, I worked in the accounting department of a medium-sized company. I was supposed to work 40 hours a week, but only about 25 hours of that week were spent doing actual work. The rest of the time I worked hard trying to keep myself entertained, and more importantly, trying to look busy.

An employee with nothing to do *has* to look busy. Otherwise, the boss will think he's redundant and will likely consider dismissing him or lowering his salary. Looking busy may be an integral part of an office employee's life, but it's inefficient, boring, and unfulfilling. Going to law school because you don't know what else to do is essentially the same thing: trying to look busy (*i.e.,* studious) about something that is quite serious (and expensive).

Many decide to go to law school because they really *can't* figure out what they want to do with their lives. Therefore, they think that if they go to law school, they can postpone the decision by a few years. This sort of cop-out is the equivalent to looking busy at the office while getting nothing done. Their law school experiences will probably be inefficient, boring, and unfulfilling. (And their experiences as attorneys are almost certain to be worse.)

One of life's hardest tasks is figuring out what to do. I can empathize with someone who is a recent college graduate and is either looking for that first job or has been working a dead-end job for a few years, and has no idea what to do next or how to get out. You feel trapped and think that going to law school will give you something to do for three years. Then, by magic, doors to prestigious and well-paying jobs will open. Wrong.

If you think you feel trapped after college, law school will just add another, *very* heavy shackle. Having a law degree might make you a more qualified job candidate than not having one—in the sense that without the joint credentials of the J.D. and successful bar exam *no* job as a lawyer is open to you—but what people don't consider is that once you graduate from law school, your options are drastically *narrowed*. On average, law students tend to graduate with a substantial amount of student-loan debt, so they have to seek jobs with salaries high enough to cover their payments. You can't just take any job you want any more, or go into any field that interests you. You're trapped all over again.

When I was a third-year law student and was thinking about what to do next, I had a million ideas for things I wanted to do— start my own business, write a book, try to get back to Europe. I was, however, due to start making payments on my student loans six *short* months after graduation.

On top of that, while I went into law school with a girlfriend, I graduated with a wife...and baby. My options were severely limited to finding a job that would pay a salary sufficient to cover our higher living expenses *and* student loan payments. It seemed that the only way I could make that kind of salary with a law degree (and little work experience) was as an entry-level attorney. The problem was that after three years of law school the only thing of which I was certain was that I didn't want to be a lawyer. Though

I didn't realize it at the time, my options after college were nearly limitless. After law school, I was nearly forced to do something I didn't want to do.

Take your time and figure out what *you* want to do. *Really* want to do. Think about your talents and think about what makes you happy. If nothing comes to mind, the best thing to do is...something else. At least for now. Work and save money instead. Try to narrow down the career possibilities to a field that truly interests you and gain as much relevant experience as possible. Don't put yourself in a position where, if you realize later what you want to do, you won't able to do it. Don't go to law school unless you're *sure* that you want to become an attorney.

My parents [spouse, friends, etc.] expect me to go. I came from a family where all the males for several generations were either doctors or engineers...or lawyers. I felt pressured to follow in their footsteps, even though I had no personal interest in any of those professions.

I grew up in Argentina, an old-fashioned country where someone's status is determined by his education and profession. I have an uncle who, like his father before him, has an engineering degree. To my knowledge, he hasn't worked a day of his life as an engineer. After he graduated, he took a job as an investment banker. He later obtained an MBA from Wharton and went on to become a successful entrepreneur.

When I was in high school, I had to make a detailed family tree for a class project. With each family member, I had to include his or her occupation. When I got to my uncle, I asked my mom what I should put down for his occupation. Without even thinking about it, she said, "He's an engineer."

I was confused. "What are you talking about? He's not an engineer. He's always talking about his business deals."

My mom insisted, "His degree is in engineering, so he's an engineer."

"But I thought he had an MBA."

"That's different. He's still an engineer."

I had a hard time believing that an engineering degree from a university in Argentina would supercede an MBA from Wharton. I compromised with my mother, and in the slot next to my uncle's name, I wrote: Engineer/entrepreneur. (Engineer had to come first though.)

While things aren't quite as old-fashioned in the United States, there is still a lot of pressure for many to pursue professional degrees. This is especially true for the sons and daughters of the highly educated. But the pressure isn't limited to people with well-educated parents. I've met many students who were the first in their families to attend college. Because of their achievements, high expectations were thrust upon them to do great things. In either case, many end up doing things they don't really want to do in order to fulfill their *families'* hopes for them.

This is your one and only life, so you shouldn't live it for the sake of others. Do what *you* want to do. If you feel pressured to go to law school, you'll feel equally if not more pressured to take an exceedingly demanding job with a competitive firm after graduation. You'll work 70 hours a week for a decade, and then 60 hours a week until you're about 70 years old when you can finally retire. By this time, the people you tried so hard to impress will all be dead. And you'll be close behind them.

You'll realize that you wasted your life studying law, writing memos, filing briefs, and doing all the things that lawyers do that you care nothing about. By this point, it will be too late to change anything. You'll die knowing you didn't live the life you wanted to live.

Also, if someone is pressuring you to go to law school, get *them* to pay for your tuition and expenses. Otherwise, you'll not only be doing something you don't want to do, but you'll be paying a fortune to do it. If someone wants you to go to law school so badly, let them pick up the tab. I doubt many people will urge you to become a lawyer if they have to cover the considerable costs.

I want to make money. There are two common stereotypes concerning lawyers: that they are evil and that they are rich. Neither of these is entirely accurate. Though I have heard countless stories of rotten attorneys, I personally know many who are genuinely nice people. Even those who are less-than-nice are often simply over-stressed, and consequently act out their frustrations. The same goes for a lawyer's level of wealth. I know attorneys who make a lot of money, but I know many others with surprisingly modest salaries. (Surprise...they're often the happier ones.)

While it's true that in this country lawyers can make a very good living, the important word is *can*. The path to becoming a wealthy attorney is an arduous one, and one that is denied to most law students. First, you must be accepted into a law school, preferably one with a national reputation (of which there are not many). A "national reputation" means, well, that everyone has at least heard about it, and if asked would say "Wow! You go *there!?*" The law school application process is a pain in the ass for all law schools, and acceptance into a top law school is *exceedingly* difficult. Once accepted, you must endure three years of boring classes, boring case books, and intensely difficult exams.

After law school, usually a few days or weeks after graduation, you then start studying for the most difficult exam known to man, the bar exam. Only after you pass the bar exam, are admitted to a state's bar, and find work can you start making money as an attorney. (Even those lucky few who have well-paying jobs waiting for them can *keep* those jobs only if they pass the bar exam.)

If you went to a good law school and got good grades or if you went to a crappy law school and got *really* good grades, you have a decent chance of making between $100,000 and $200,000 a year. (Actually, that's not quite true. If you go to a crappy law school and are in the top ten or even five percent of the class *and* the economy is strong...you've got a chance. Otherwise, forget it. No high-powered job, no big bucks. Just student loan payments.) Chances are, you will probably make between $50,000 and $100,000 a year, depending on who hires you—or even less if you take a job with the government or a small firm.

Still, don't think that it's smooth sailing once you start getting paid. Law firms don't just give money away. In short, you have to work your ass off. The more you get paid, the harder you have to work; not the other way around. Attorneys do *not* work nine to five. Expect to work at least 50-60 hours a week if you're hired by a smaller firm. If you're "lucky" enough to land a big firm job, then expect to work *at least* 60-70 hours a week. Yes, attorneys can make good money, but they earn every penny. So if you're going to law school for the sole reason of making money, then you should save yourself the hassle and find an easier and more enjoyable way to achieve that goal.

On average, corporate executives make significantly more money than attorneys. Physicians earn similar salaries as attorneys, but after their first few years they don't seem to work as intensely. Dentists definitely don't seem to work as hard. Engineers make good salaries and aren't necessarily required to obtain graduate degrees. Stock brokers, investment bankers, and real estate brokers can make a killing, and, though common, they don't even really need a bachelor's degree. They just have to know what they're doing, pass an exam, and impress someone in a job interview. Many of the world's most successful entrepreneurs have no more than a high school diploma.

Law school requires a significant investment of time and money. When I graduated law school, I found myself to be over $100,000 in debt. The old adage that you have to spend money to make money is for the most part true. But if money is your main concern, then there are many better ways to invest $100,000 than in a law degree. You could use that money to start a business, or invest in securities or real estate. At least that way you have a potential return on your money. A law degree is only worth anything if you put it to work. That means putting *yourself* to work, *as an attorney.* Otherwise you'll be six figures in debt with only a piece of paper to show for it. Diploma frame not included.

I could do anything with a law degree. I hate résumés. There is much more to a person than a list of qualifications on a piece of paper. Still, the job market revolves around résumés, and in order to get a job, or even an interview, you must impress employers with a good one.

Many go to law school not really wanting to become attorneys, but searching for a nice addition to their résumés. Although they won't directly say they want to use their law degree as a résumé booster, they go to law school with the impression that a law degree will help them land a good job in business, politics, or just about anywhere. A hundred thousand dollars is an awful lot to pay for an extra line on a piece of paper.

Having gone through law school, if I were hiring someone for a non-law job, I would give a great deal of merit to a law degree on someone's résumé. However, this merit would lie solely on the premise that the person must be pretty smart, or at least disciplined, after completing three grueling years of law school. I would not hire that person with the idea that the education they attained in law school would be a benefit to the company. Many others would instantly discount such an applicant, because the application would make no sense: why hire a law school graduate for a job not requiring law practice? What's *wrong* with this person anyway?

The law school curriculum is designed to teach students fundamental elements of American law so that they may become attorneys and possibly judges. It will not, however, prepare one for a career outside the law. Although you will learn many valuable things that will make for useful personal knowledge, a law degree does not gives its holder an educational advantage over another job candidate if the position isn't law related.

Required courses such as Torts, Civil Procedure, or Constitutional Law will be nearly useless to someone not wanting to practice law. You might recall in high school when every student who was bad at math would say, "Math is worthless. I'm never going to use it." Unless you intend to practice law, however, you *can* safely say this about most law school classes. Math really *is* useful, but the Rule Against Perpetuities?

Other courses such as Contracts or Corporations might give you an advantage in a business job. Maybe. But in that case, a candidate with an MBA is more qualified for the position, having devoted a mere two years to the study of business. (And there are many hungry MBAs looking for work.)

A law degree is necessary only if you want to practice law. To *be* an attorney. I know of no other job in the world where a law degree is required. Therefore, if you want to add some bulk to your résumé, there are plenty of more enjoyable and affordable options. After all, you don't hear about people going to medical school hoping to land a job in, say, politics.

One other element that employers look for is experience. (Whether you're good or bad, loved it or hated it, is irrelevant. What's important in sifting through stacks of résumés is that you actually *did* it.) Identify the line of work that most interests you and try to obtain experience related to it, even if you have to start at the very bottom as a low-level employee or unpaid intern. So, do what you love. Seriously. The more experience in a particular area that you have under your belt, the more doors will open for you—and the more of a vested interest you have in continuing in that line of work.

In the three years it would take you to complete law school, you could notch three valuable years of experience—plus three years of a salary, 401(k), and benefits. Employers will be happy to hire you knowing that they will not have to spend time and money training you. If all you have is a law degree, but you have never stepped foot inside an office, you'd better be prepared to convince your employer that it would be worth his while to hire you and spend several months training you before you can become productive. If it's not even a job in the law, you're flat-out barking up the wrong tree.

Another way to boost your résumé is in learning a foreign language. Currently, employees fluent in Spanish or Chinese are coveted by businesses. You could spend three years in China or Mexico studying the language and living like a king for a few dollars a day. (And, often, getting paid a modest salary with housing benefits as an English teacher. Or there's always the Peace Corps— an experience if ever there was one.) Nearly all who have done any of these speak highly of their experience abroad. For those who don't want to practice law, it is almost certainly a better, more enjoyable, more affordable, and more worthwhile experience than three years of law school. (Even if you do want to practice law, this can still be beneficial: such experience can make the difference in acceptance to a top law school.)

Think about what you're interested in and what you *really* want to do. Then, think about specific ways in which you can make yourself more suitable for success in that area. If you go to law school hoping to obtain an impressive general degree, then you will waste your time and your money (unless you are lucky enough to have someone else paying for it, in which case you'll waste only three years of your life). Afterward, you might have a better résumé than you had before, but you won't have as good a résumé as you could have had.

Be honest with yourself. When I was going through the application process, a family friend came over for dinner and I told him about my intentions of going to law school. He was surprised about my decision. "Really? Law school?!" he commented, "You never really struck me as the lawyer type. I thought you would end up in a more creative field."

He had studied business and had a good managerial job at a big corporation. As a hobby on the side, he dabbled in poetry. When he learned that I was an English major—as if that meant anything— he took the liberty of making me his personal poetry coach. He would show me his poems, complete with forced rhymes and obvious metaphors, and he would ask me what I thought. I would have to think about death to keep from laughing in his face.

Bored with his choice, he had looked to me to vicariously live his life again. He had bypassed a career as a failed poet for a lucrative one in the corporate world. He regretted this, and when he saw that I might be following in his footsteps, he was disappointed.

"Why do you want to go to law school?"

He asked a perfectly legitimate question, but I became defensive trying to think of a good answer. "Well," I said, not believing the words that came out of my mouth, "I feel that with a law degree, I would be able to do important things. Good things that I could be proud of. I could help people. Change the world for the better."

He wasn't convinced. I wasn't either. The truth is that there were plenty of perfectly good things I could have been doing. There were plenty of people I could've been helping. I had just never bothered to. There was no way a law degree was going to change that. He knew this. I should've known it too.

If you're contemplating going to law school, think about the reasons why you want go. Be *honest* with yourself. If you're truly interested in the law and you want a career as an attorney, then you have my blessing to go to law school (as if that mattered). I hope my experience and the advice in this book will be at least somewhat helpful to you.

If your reasons for going to law school are impure, I suggest you think *seriously* about your decision. For me, it's too late. But you can learn from my mistakes. If you're not absolutely convinced, after serious thought and for the right reasons...don't go to law school. Get out while you still can.

2

THE APPLICATION

If the last chapter didn't do its job to dissuade you, and you still want to go to law school, then the next step to consider is the application process. This isn't like applying for a job at McDonald's, where you fill out an application, talk to the manager for fifteen minutes, and start on Monday. Applying to law school is a *long* process. It takes (seemingly) forever; requires a great deal of effort filled with plentiful details, ancillary materials, and follow-up; is quite expensive; and, for nearly all, includes a healthy dose of bad news. Even before you hear the results, it is, in short, a pain in the ass. In these senses this process is a fitting prelude to what's ahead once you actually start law school.

Ideally, you should allot *one year* to complete the application process. This means that you can't decide that you want to go to law school on the day of your college graduation in May and hope to start classes in August. If you decide to go to law school in May, plan to start classes in August of the *following* year.

Each school has its own deadlines, and depending on how fast you can get things done, you can probably complete the process in a few months. Give yourself a year to get everything done, so you can space the requirements out and not feel rushed or stressed out. You'll then be finished with everything early enough so you'll have plenty of time before law school starts. For example, you could devote a week to an admissions essay, and do a little bit of work on it each day. The next week could be devoted to obtaining letters of recommendation, and so on. Otherwise, you'll be doing a million things at once, and it will feel like your life revolves around getting into law school. If you can't handle the stress of the application process, then you'll hate law school. Quit now while you're ahead and you haven't made any tuition payments.

In case you're curious, a bit of personal background: I decided to go to law school in July. I started working on the application process in late August, took the LSAT in October, and sent all my applications out by December. I got responses back as early as

January and as late as August. (I was even waiting to hear back from a school when I started classes.) By April, I was so sick of thinking about law school that I quit my job, gave my parents proxy authority to sign forms on my behalf, and went to France for a wonderful three-month vacation. This luxury would have been impossible had I not allotted sufficient time to the application process. I was able to start law school relaxed and with a fresh head.

If you can, you should try to plan the application process so that other responsibilities don't interfere. For example, if you have a demanding job that takes up nearly all of your thinking time, you will need to seriously plan your schedule. You'll need a generous amount of free time to study for the LSAT, especially. Applying to law school—if you decide to do so—should be a high if not your first priority. If you try instead to wing the application process and go on with your regularly scheduled life—as served you well in your past college life—you might well sacrifice your chances of entry at a law school that would be a better fit for you.

At the same time, you should also be careful not to let the application process interfere too much with your other responsibilities. Many apply to law school during their final year of college. Be careful not to concentrate all your efforts on applying to law school and forget your current classes. If the application process causes your GPA to suffer, it will be counterproductive. A few points on your GPA can make a big difference on whether certain law schools accept you. If you work, be careful not to neglect your duties in favor of the application process. It will be pretty hard to get your boss to write you a letter of recommendation if he fired you the week before.

When I was applying to law school, I had the perfect set-up. I took an accounting job at an office where I had interned as a college student. My old boss emailed me while I was traveling abroad, and told me that the current accountant was leaving the office in a few weeks and someone was needed to replace him. Since he remembered me fondly from my days as an intern, he thought of me and offered me the job.

By this point, I had already decided I wanted to go to law school, so I was wary about taking what appeared to be a fairly serious job. I thought back to my days as an intern. I remembered that about

85% of my time at the office was spent screwing around on the internet, writing emails, and playing computer solitaire. Though I worked 40 hours a week, I was actually given relatively little work to complete. I would quickly finish my work, and then practically stare at the wall until quitting time. I thought that if this job was anything like that internship, it would be perfect. I would have time to work on my law school applications, and I would get paid.

I went in to meet with my old boss and told him that I would love to take the job, but only for a year since I was planning on attending law school. Having gone to law school himself, he thought it was great that I was following in his footsteps. I was thus hired on an interim basis, and was supposed to work there up until a few days before law school started. However, working nine to five in an Indianapolis office proved to be even duller than I had expected. After seven months, I quit the job and took that three month vacation in France.

While it lasted, the job was ideal. I had plenty of free time as well as access to anything I could possibly need for working on the application process: high speed internet, a good computer, a printer, a copy machine, and a fax machine. It was like having my own little office for the purpose of applying to law school. Any time I had no work to do—which was often—I worked on the application process. I researched schools, wrote the essays, worked on my résumé, requested the letters of recommendation, filled out and submitted the applications, and even studied for the LSAT. It seemed as if applying to law school was part of my job. Believe me, getting paid to apply to law school makes the whole application process much easier to stomach. Finding such a position is well worth the trouble, if you can.

THE LSAT

In their websites and pamphlets, law schools proclaim that for their admissions process they consider each applicant individually, looking at their entire application and considering all factors. That's misleading, at best. Admissions offices weed applicants out by their LSAT scores and GPA, considering other factors only if the applicant's score is high enough. The most important part of the application process is thus the LSAT exam, and the score you get will be the biggest determinant of which law schools will accept and which will reject you.

This system doesn't seem very fair, but it *is* understandable. After all, admissions offices receive far more applications than they have staff to read them, and they simply don't have time to carefully read every essay and every résumé. They need a concrete, objective device that will differentiate applicants with some reasonable degree of accuracy. That leaves them with an applicant's LSAT score and undergraduate grade point average. Notably, an applicant's college GPA is trickier because it can be assumed that most people applying to law school did pretty well as undergrads, so the thousands of applicants are probably going to have similar GPAs. Plus, you have to take into account the competitiveness of an applicant's university, and whether his major was an impressive one like Physics or a less-impressive one like, say, Physical Education.

Therefore, I hate to break the news to you, but your LSAT score will be *the* deciding factor on whether you'll get into the law school you've been dreaming about. If you get a great score on the exam that places you well above-average for that school, then you can tell the admissions people to go to hell in your admissions essay (though you probably shouldn't). Chances are they probably won't even read it. They'll just see your LSAT score and toss your application packet in the "Accepted" pile. If you get a terrible LSAT score, then you could probably tell them to go to hell just the same, because it won't matter what you write. If your LSAT score sucks, you could write the great American novel and you still wouldn't get in.

Most admissions departments are kind enough to provide data about what LSAT score you'll need to be accepted. Reader-friendly charts show the scores and grades that made up the 75th and 25th percentiles of all the students who were accepted. By plugging in your own LSAT score and GPA, you can get a pretty accurate idea of what your chances of acceptance would be at that law school. Admissions departments are married to these charts. If you get a 158, and it doesn't seem that the school you like admits anyone with an LSAT score under 165, it won't matter if you found the cure for cancer; you're probably not getting in.

I took the LSAT only once and I was most disappointed with my score, a meager 156. Some recommended that I take it again, but I didn't think it was necessary. I thought that even if my LSAT score was low for the schools I liked, I had other fine qualities to offer. I believed the admissions departments when they said they considered each applicant individually and weighed all the factors. Other than my LSAT score, I felt that I was a competitive applicant: I had a 3.7 GPA, graduated college in three and a half years with a competitive major and two minors, am fluent in four languages, had some decent work experience, had traveled all over Europe and South America, and had (I thought) good letters of recommendation and essays. On top of all that, I'm a member of a minority population. (Even though I'm 6'-3" with light skin and blue eyes, both my parents are Latin American and I grew up in Argentina.) Surely, I thought, the law schools I liked would overlook my weak LSAT score. They couldn't possibly reject such a qualified minority applicant.

I was wrong. As the responses arrived in the mail, they were all true to the admissions charts. All of the schools for which my LSAT score was below the acceptance line rejected me. And all the schools for which my LSAT score was above the acceptance line accepted me. It was as simple as that.

I understand that admissions departments have to resort to an objective figure to weed out applicants. What I don't understand is why they decided on the LSAT. Perhaps I'm bitter, but I think the LSAT is an absolutely terrible indicator of whether someone will succeed in law school. The exam consists of little logic games and reading comprehension exercises that do not in the least bit resemble what a law student does in law school. Of all the exams I took in law school, none came close to even resembling the LSAT. I don't understand why law schools accept or reject applicants based on their performance on a completely arbitrary exam. They might as well have arm-wrestling contests and accept the applicants with the strongest forearms.

One of my good friends from law school got an abysmal score on his LSAT. It was probably one of the lowest scores our law school accepted that year. All the top-tier schools to which he applied rejected him, even though he had a great GPA from an Ivy League university. In law school, my friend managed to get excellent grades. He took a spot at the top of our class, and for his second year, he transferred to one of the schools that had rejected him the year before. By the time law school ended, he had a great job waiting for him at a big, competitive firm. His LSAT score was a grossly inaccurate measure of how he would perform in law school.

So if you're upset about getting a bad LSAT score, don't worry. Even though you might not get into the school of your choice, you shouldn't interpret it as an indicator that you'll do poorly in law school.

LSAT Prep Courses. Even though the LSAT may be irrelevant to your eventual success as a law student, it is still the most important part of the application process, so you have no choice but to approach it seriously and study hard for it. Various courses are offered to help you prepare for the LSAT. The most popular ones are offered by Kaplan and Princeton Review. From those I have spoken with who enrolled in these courses, their responses on whether they found them to be helpful or not are mixed. Not to say that these courses aren't helpful; surely, at the very least, they give you some instruction on how to approach the problems, and they give you plenty of practice tests to do in class or at home. One thing that is certain is that these courses are expensive. Therefore, the most common response I get from people who took these courses is: *"Yes, it was helpful; but no, it wasn't worth the hefty price tag."*

The decision is up to you. If money is not a big issue, and you can afford the course, then it might be worth it. It certainly won't hurt you and you might maximize your score by a few crucial points. If you decide that the course is too expensive and you would rather study on your own and have enough money left over to, say, buy a used car or take a nice vacation, that's fine too. It's possible to study on your own and get a good score. The most important thing, whether you enroll in a course or not, is that you study as much as you can on your own time.

My LSAT score was lousy, so feel free to ignore any or all of my advice. However, it might be good for you to learn from my mistakes and try not to repeat them. My first mistake was enrolling in a bad course. I decided that the Kaplan and Princeton Review courses were too expensive, so instead I enrolled in a bargain-basement course offered by a local university. It cost about $200, and only met once a week for a month, but it still ended up being worse than a complete waste of my money and time. The teacher was an old, bitter attorney who used the course as a soapbox to tell bad jokes and exaggerated stories about how hard the life of a lawyer was. He didn't really teach anything about how to approach the LSAT problems. He just gave trite pieces of advice that everybody knew, such as: "If you don't know a problem, skip it and come back to it at the end."

It wasn't my fault that my teacher sucked, but it *was* my fault that I did no preliminary research on what the course would consist of, or what I was getting into. I just signed up for it because it was about six times cheaper than any of the other courses. So if you're thinking about taking an LSAT course, do your research. Look into it and find out everything you can about it. Otherwise, like me, you might end up wasting your time and money.

Find out who will be teaching the course. Will it be an old attorney who took the LSAT fifty years ago and hasn't seen a copy of an exam since? Will it be some kid who just took the LSAT for the first time a few months ago? I had a friend in law school who was hired to teach a course on the same year he took the LSAT for the first time. I asked him what he had gotten on his LSAT and, though he had gotten a higher score than mine, it was hardly high enough to qualify him as an LSAT expert. Inquire about who will be teaching the course and decide for yourself whether the teacher is worthy of your time and money.

Even more important than having access to a good teacher is having access to good practice tests. Included in the tuition for the course I took was an LSAT textbook that included several practice tests. This was the best part of the course. Every night, I did a different practice test, timing myself to simulate the actual LSAT exam. As the day of the exam neared, and I was finishing up the last of the practice tests, I was getting really good at the problems. I would get very few wrong, and for the ones I did get wrong I could quickly figure out what my mistake had been after a second look. When I tallied up the points for my mock LSAT exams, I kept getting great scores. I was convinced that I would kick ass when the time came for the actual LSAT.

On the last day of this worthless course—a week before the LSAT—one of my classmates raised her hand and asked: "How will the problems on the LSAT compare to the ones in our textbook?" The professor, acting as if this wasn't something he might've mentioned earlier, answered: "Oh, the actual LSAT problems will be *much* harder." Half the class looked shocked; the other half looked angry.

The whole time, I had assumed that the practice tests were actual LSAT problems from past exams, or at the very least, fairly accurate replicas. That night, when I got home, I looked up an old LSAT exam on the internet. At least my teacher had been right about one thing—the legitimate old exams I found online were a hell of a lot harder than the practice tests I had been taking. With only a few days before I was scheduled to take the LSAT, my confidence was shot. I managed to look at a few of the old exams, but I just didn't have enough time. When it came time for the LSAT, I was under-prepared and unsure of what to expect.

My advice is to get as many good practice tests as possible. Do as many as you can, as often as you can, and for as long as you can before the LSAT. Supposedly, if you enroll in the Kaplan or Princeton Review courses, you get access to old LSAT exams and accurate practice tests. That alone might be worth enrolling in one of those courses.

On the other hand, if you decide to bypass a course and study on your own, you can find plenty of practice tests and old exams online. Also, go to the library and get as many LSAT books as possible. The key is to diversify; don't do what I did and work from a single book. If you take enough practice exams—good and accurate ones—you'll know exactly what to expect on exam day and you won't be surprised by anything.

Relax. My final piece of advice is that you relax. *Try* not to stress yourself out. Recently, a friend of mine, who went against my counsel and insisted on applying to law school, developed a monomaniacal obsession with the LSAT. He turned down a job offer from a pharmaceutical company and quit playing in his beloved garage band—devastating the other members of the band and all three of their fans—to devote all of his time to studying for the LSAT. He signed up to take it in October, and after taking one of the expensive prep courses and studying for months he got cold feet, decided he wasn't ready, and postponed it until December instead. Never breaking his stride, he kept on studying full-time, and when the fateful day arrived he was perfectly ready, though entirely too nervous.

Apparently, in the exam room, an inconsiderate proctor decided to use that time to write emails to everyone he knew, and so he typed noisily while my friend and the other test-takers tried to concentrate. I don't know just how loud or distracting a computer keyboard can be—it's not like it was one of those old-fashioned typewriters—but it was too much for my friend to handle. It took him about 15 minutes to work up the nerve to say something, and when he did, not wanting to contribute to the noise, he stood up and flapped his arms around trying to get the proctor's attention. When the proctor noticed him, he and my friend got into a heated exchange of silent hand signaling: "Why are you flapping your arms?" "Never mind me, why are *you* typing on the computer?"

By the time the conflict was resolved, my friend was certain that it had been enough of a distraction to cause him to bomb the test. So when he got home, he decided to file a formal complaint against the proctor, and cancel his score. If you feel that you performed poorly, you have the option of canceling your score, and neither you nor any law schools to which you apply will know how you did. The reason this option is available is that law schools aren't forgiving if you happen to have a bad day. Even if you take the LSAT a second time and get a perfect score, law schools will still see your lower score, and quite possibly use it against you. It's kind of like a game of high-stakes poker—you can cancel your score (fold) and live to play another round; or take your chances and wait for your score (hit me), knowing that a bad card will ruin your hand.

The problem with the option of canceling your score is that you can't do it forever. In order to submit a completed application, you'll have to, at some point, submit an LSAT score, even if it's not as high as you'd like it to be. My friend's dilemma was that, since he had chickened out of the October test and cancelled his December score, he was left with a do-or-die scenario in February. This would be his last chance to take the LSAT and submit a score in time (and even this is pushing it), or he would have to wait another year before starting law school. Having been nervous enough for his two prior attempts, his anxiety level now rose to a degree high enough to contribute to global warming. After more than six months of studying, he could figure out a logic game in his sleep. His obstacle was his anxiety.

The day before the test, he drove to the test center to familiarize himself with it. He figured out the best route to get there, where to park, and how much time to allot to such logistical measures. At night, he prepared what clothes to wear, what to eat for breakfast, and what to bring to the test. I don't suppose he slept very well, but nevertheless, he was up and ready when the morning came. He arrived on time, determined to not let any little distractions get to him like the last time. Today was his day.

Or so it seemed, until a lady at the check-in counter politely asked him, "Could I see some picture I.D. please?" He reached into the back pocket of his jeans, but all he could feel was his butt-cheek; he had forgotten his wallet. This guy always carried his wallet around; it went with him everywhere but the shower. But the LSAT played dirty tricks on his mind—it made him doubt his abilities in October, be distracted by a computer keyboard in December, and forget his driver's license in February.

Driving without a license would have been the least of his worries had a cop pulled him over as he sped home, running red lights, barely dodging other cars and pedestrians. When he arrived home, he kicked the front door open, nearly killing his parents of simultaneous heart attacks as they peacefully ate breakfast. Without a single word of explanation—except for a barrage of curse words—he ran upstairs to his room and got what he was looking for. He then hurried back outside and drove off, leaving smoke and tire marks in the suburban cul-de-sac that was just starting to wake up.

Miraculously, nobody was killed, injured, or arrested, and my friend managed to squeeze into a seat as the proctor read off the test instructions. However, it took him the duration of the first section to catch his breath, and the duration of the second section to stop being so angry at himself for his absentmindedness. Once again, it was enough of a distraction to sabotage his performance, and he claims he would have cancelled his score again, had he not been at the end of the line. He was right; when he got his score back, it was disappointing.

What was even more frustrating than his score was that he had wasted half a year studying for a single test, and now he was walking away unsatisfied. People don't study that much for even the bar exam. He probably would have gotten a similar score had he just gone ahead and taken it in October, or waited to see his score in December. He became obsessed with the LSAT and let his nerves get the best of him. Still, all that suffering ended up being moot. Even with his low score, he got accepted into a few good schools, and ended up happy with his ultimate choice. Now, he thinks back to his crazy LSAT experiences and laughs. While the LSAT is important, if you dwell too much on its importance, it will ultimately hurt you. Approach it seriously, but relax; excessive stress or anxiety will only hinder your performance.

WHICH SCHOOLS SHOULD YOU APPLY TO

After you get your LSAT sore, you should have a general idea of what schools will be likely to accept you. Now is the time to narrow them down and decide which ones to apply to. You can apply to as many schools as you like, but remember that application fees usually range between $50 and $100. So if you apply to every top-tier school hoping to maximize your odds of acceptance, it will cost you a fortune. (And, unless your LSAT and GPA put you in the top few percent, as mentioned you're wasting your hopes as well as your money.) You might get rejected by every school and you will retrospectively regret your strategy.

I recommend that you divide schools into three categories: Dream Schools, Target Schools, and Safety Schools.

Dream Schools. These are schools you would love to attend, but getting into them is a long shot. By "long shot," I mean that your scores are at the bottom of the data for students regularly accepted at that school.

Target Schools. These are schools you would (or should) be happy to attend. You have a realistic chance of acceptance, but it's not quite a sure shot. This means that your LSAT score and GPA place you somewhere in the middle of regularly accepted applicants.

Safety Schools. These are schools you are fairly certain you can get into, because your LSAT/GPA are at or above the high end of the stats for that school. You might not be too excited about attending, but if all else fails, at least you'll have somewhere to go.

Depending on how many applications you intend to submit, and how much money you want to spend on non-refundable application fees, narrow your schools down to a handful in each category. The best strategy is to concentrate primarily on target schools, but leaving room for one or two dream schools and one or two safety schools (For example, you could apply to four target schools, two dream schools, and two safety schools.)

Be realistic, and keep your ego in check. If you overestimate yourself, you will end up wasting a lot of money on application fees and getting back a bunch of rejection letters. Trust me, even if it's from a shot-in-the-dark dream school, rejection letters *hurt.* On the other hand, don't sell yourself short. You might end up missing out and not going to a law school you could have gotten into. If you look at the admissions charts and plug in your LSAT score and GPA, you should have a pretty good idea of what schools you can get into.

After you've narrowed it down to a few schools, what's left is to fill out the applications, send everything in, and wait. They say waiting is the hardest part. It isn't; it's actually pretty easy. It's out of your hands at that point.

3

Choosing a Law School

After deciding to go to law school, choosing which school to attend is the most important decision you'll make during the law school application process. It's important in the sense that if you make the wrong decision you could end up being miserable for at least three years, and quite possibly far longer.

One upside to having a competitive admissions process is that your choice of law school is limited to the law schools that will accept you. (Unless, of course, you're one of those obnoxious geniuses who can get in anywhere. In that case, your biggest dilemma is whether you should sacrifice the old-money prestige of Harvard or Yale for the favorable weather at Stanford.) The challenge for everyone else is how to decide—among those schools that are within your grasp—which to attend.

LAW SCHOOL RANKINGS

The most obvious suggestion is to go to the best school that accepts you. But who determines whether one school is better than another? For some mysterious reason, the magazine *U.S. News & World Report* has inherited this responsibility. Every year, it authoritatively announces which law schools are better than which. It ranks each and every accredited law school in the country, making it easy for law students and professors to accurately know just how proud of themselves and their achievements they should be.

Academic authorities, such as law school deans or university presidents, frequently denounce the *U.S. News* rankings. They say that they are irrelevant and should be disregarded. If you hear a dean say this, it means that his school did poorly in that year's ranking. If that school jumps up in the ranking, you can bet that the same dean will brag about it in the next brochure for prospective students.

The rankings bode well for the schools that rank highly (or that rise) and make life miserable for the schools that don't (or that fall).

In reality, the *U.S. News* rankings are not "official." They're based on a formula and are published by a journalistic, non-academic magazine. It's roughly the equivalent of *People* magazine's *50 Most Beautiful People.* (Well, not quite, but still it's hardly the exact science that it's presented to be—and taken as.) The truth, for good or bad, is that anyone involved in any way with any law school knows about these rankings…and pays attention to them.

Every law student in the country knows where his school ranks and has a pretty good idea of where other schools stand as well. When law students from different law schools meet, they instantly know where they stand in the pecking order. If you ask someone from the top-tiered University of Michigan Law School what law school he goes to, he will stand tall and announce the name of his school proudly: "I go to *Michigan!*" (He might add, "…people call it the Harvard of the Midwest.") On the other hand, when asked the same question, someone from the fourth-tiered Detroit College of Law will slouch and inaudibly mumble: "Detroit College of Law." If challenged he might add, "…it's accredited."

This is unfortunate. As the Beach Boys sang, "be true to your school." No matter what law school you go to, you should be proud of it. And if it doesn't rank very highly, just do what the deans do— tell everyone the *U.S. News* rankings are full of crap.

There are reasons other than pride, however, to pay attention to the *U.S. News* rankings. Law students aren't the only ones who know how schools rank. Law firms keep a close eye on the rankings and are deeply influenced by them when hiring new associates. Just as the LSAT makes life easier for admissions officers by weeding out applicants, the *U.S. News* rankings make life easier for law firm recruiters by weeding out job applicants. All a recruiter has to do to know which law schools to hire from is look inside a magazine. This means that if the school you go to doesn't rank well, you might have to hustle a little more—or a *lot* more—to find a job. And if you're that obnoxious genius from Harvard, you'll be swatting recruiters away like flies. (You can use a rolled-up issue of *U.S. News* to swat at them.)

Thus, even though I would love to tell you to ignore the rankings and find the school that is the best fit for you, I can't. You should at least glance at the rankings and have an idea of where a school ranks before you commit to going there. But while ignoring the rankings would be a mistake, placing too much emphasis on them is wrong as well. First of all, don't be discouraged. I've heard some approach the application process saying, "If I don't get into a good school, I'm not going to law school." If true, that person is going to law school for the wrong reasons. As I wrote in the first chapter, the only good reason to go to law school is to become an attorney. No matter where a school ranks—whether it's first or last—its graduates can practice law in any of the fifty United States, as long as it's accredited by the American Bar Association.

Also, going to a low-ranked school doesn't mean you can't have a successful career as an attorney. You might have to jump a few more hurdles early in your career, but if you're a good attorney and you win cases, nobody will care what law school you attended. (This is true in litigation especially.) Earlier, I somewhat mocked the Detroit College of Law. However, I'll have you know that one of my favorite professors during law school was a graduate of the very same Detroit College of Law. He was an accomplished attorney in his field and a highly knowledgeable professor. He made plenty of money and never chased an ambulance. He was, in short, the type of attorney most of us should aspire to be—and it didn't take a Harvard Law School diploma.

One thing you should keep in mind about the *U.S. News* rankings is that they're fickle. Certain law schools have fairly secure spots on the grid. For example, while Harvard and Yale often fight for the first and second spots, you can pretty safely bet three years' worth of tuition money that neither of the two will leave the top tier—or even the top ten—anytime soon. However, as you go lower in the rankings, schools can jump one or more spots in either direction from year to year.

When I was applying to law school, *U.S. News* only provided individual rankings for the first tier. For the second, third, and fourth tiers, the schools were simply listed alphabetically in their respective tier. As I was weighing my options, I chose one school over another because it was a second-tier school, while the other was in the third tier, even though the third-tier school offered me a generous scholarship of $10,000.00.

The very next year, when the new rankings came out, it appeared that *U.S. News* had decided to put in the extra effort and individually rank the second-tier schools as well as the first. The good news was that my school was still in the second tier and the school whose offer I had rejected was still in the third. The bad news was that my school was ranked at the very end of the second tier. There was no way I could have known this the year before.

During my second year at my chosen law school, my worst nightmare came true: You guessed it—my law school drifted downward, into the third tier. No one knew what had happened. There had been no major changes at the school; the professors and the administration were all the same. I guess the new first year class must have been pretty dumb. Or maybe last year's graduates bombed the bar exam. I don't know what it was, but all of a sudden, we had gotten a whole tier worse. "Damn," I thought, "I should've taken the scholarship money."

Fortunately, when the rankings came out during my third year, my school had jumped back into the second tier. I breathed a sigh of relief, but I knew not to get too excited. You never know where your school will end up.

Almost as easily and randomly as a school can drop in the rankings, it can also go up. During the application process, when I was considering what schools to apply to, I took a close look at the University of Miami's School of Law. I liked the city of Miami, and I could see myself living there. I fantasized about living in a condo in South Beach and going out to the clubs every night. In a less decadent sense, I also liked how the school catered to Spanish-speaking students. I seriously thought about going there, but according to the *U.S. News* rankings, it was an unremarkable third-tier school. Ignorantly, I considered the school to be beneath me and decided not to apply.

As it turned out, the very next year—you guessed it—Miami moved up to the second tier, only a few spots behind the law school I did attend. The year after that, it skyrocketed up to the top half of the second tier, at least fifty slots ahead of my school. "Damn," I thought, "I should've gone to Miami." But who knows? Had I attended Miami, it might have instead slid downward into the fourth tier.

As you can see, the *U.S. News* rankings can be unpredictable. It's not a completely reliable source, and if you rely on it too heavily, you could end up picking the wrong law school. In my case, those *#&*$! rankings cost me $30,000.00 in scholarship money and three years of living in South Beach.

My advice is that you should only resort to the rankings to pick between schools if there's a significant difference in their rankings. For example, if you get into a first-tier school that has been in the first tier for a long time and shows no signs of slipping in the future, it might be worth it to pick that school over one that is perpetually ranked in the second tier.

Then again, it's not always wise to choose a school simply because it's a top-tier school. I once asked one of my good friends from law school what schools he had applied to, and he named about seven schools. Six of the schools were in California; the seventh was the University of Iowa's College of Law. I was absolutely baffled and asked him: "Why the hell did you apply to *Iowa?*"

"Well," he explained, "it was one of the few first-tier schools I thought I could get into."

This guy was willing to spend three years in, well, *Iowa*, just because it's ranked in the first tier. I'm sure it's a great school, but I've driven through Iowa, and it was like being in a black hole with the lights on (and this is coming from someone who lived in Indiana)

There *are* things more important than how a school ranks. It would be nice to have a diploma from a top-tier school, but keep in mind that law school will consume three years of your life. Are you willing to spend three years freezing your ass off in a cornfield because some magazine survey thinks highly of a certain school? Fortunately for my friend, Iowa rejected him.

LOCATION, LOCATION, LOCATION

I chose which law schools to apply to and which one to attend almost exclusively because of location. While I'm not encouraging you to follow in my footsteps—in fact, I would advise against that—a school's location is among the most important factors to consider.

As you might recall from the first chapter, I decided to go to law school as an excuse to move to Hawaii. Unfortunately, even though my scores appeared to be good enough, the University of Hawaii's School of Law rejected me. I guess over the years, Hawaii's admissions department has developed a pretty good bullshit detector, learning to differentiate the serious applicants (*i.e.,* Hawaii locals, or at least applicants with *some* legitimate connection to the islands) from the potential beach bums (*i.e.,* anyone from the mainland just looking for a few years on the beach).

Other than Hawaii, I decided to apply to schools in California and New York. I figured that not only would it be fun to go to school in either place, but if I had to take the bar exam and work there the rest of my life, it might as well be in a state that wouldn't bore me to death. In the end, I had to decide between the two best schools that had accepted me. They were similar as far as reputation and ranking. The main difference between them was that one was in California and the other in New York City. I was torn. I had always dreamed of living in Manhattan, but California had sunshine and nice beaches, just like Hawaii (well, *almost* just like Hawaii).

After it was all said and done, the deciding factor for me was the weather. It had been a particularly brutal winter in Indiana. (Come to think of it, every winter in the Midwest is particularly brutal.) I had never been to New York in the winter, but I'd heard it was pretty cold there too. Why freeze when I could stay warm and have a nice tan year-round? So, I decided to go to law school in beautiful, sunny California.

In one sense, going to law school in California worked out quite well for me. Coming from the geographically dull and meteorologically challenged Midwest, I quickly fell in love with California, making the most of its amazing weather and landscapes. I took up surfing, cycling, and snowboarding, and went on several road-trips up and down the state. In fact, if law school hadn't interfered, it probably would have been the greatest three years of my life.

In a more responsible, career-oriented sense, going to law school in California did not work out as well as I would have liked. This was mostly due to my brilliant decision to move across the country after graduation and try to find a law job in Florida. Yes, I had my reasons. My wife, whom I married during my second year of law school, is from Florida, and with a new baby—born during my ("our") third year—we wanted to be closer to family. Also, while for me California is—hands down—the most beautiful state in the Union (except, of course, for Hawaii), it's priced as if it were the most beautiful place in the universe. It's great to have the option of surfing in the ocean and skiing in the mountains on the same day, but for the price of a modest house in an unremarkable suburb in the Bay Area or Los Angeles, you could buy a beach condo in Florida *and* a chalet in the Canadian Rockies.

So it was off to Florida, where I pretty much had to start from zero to find a job. I went to a fairly small private school that is well-recognized in California, but little known away from the West Coast. No Florida firms recruited at my law school—only firms from California and a handful from nearby Western states. There were no alumni from my school practicing in Florida—most stayed in California, with a few exceptions practicing in random states. The most devastating part was that upon arriving in Florida, it seemed that many hadn't even *heard* of my law school.

The golden rule when choosing a law school is thus to go to school in the vicinity of where you want to practice. All of a sudden, this puts a lot more pressure on you. Not only do you have to pick which law school to attend for the next three years, you have to pick where you're going to live and work until you die or retire—whichever comes first. Let's not be overly dramatic; you can still move to another jurisdiction. It will just be harder for you to find that first job and get your foot in the door. Still, if you know—or have a rough idea—where you would like to live and work for the rest of your life, then find a law school within that vicinity.

Of course, there's an exception to this golden rule: if you get into a really good school. Graduates from Harvard don't have to worry about being confined to practicing law in Massachusetts. The whole world is in demand for Harvard grads. Then again, just because a school is ranked in the top tier, it doesn't mean you can walk into a law firm on the other side of the country and impress everyone.

For example, let's consider the University of Iowa again. Indeed, it's a well-regarded, top-tier school, and its graduates will be likely to find jobs outside of Iowa with relative ease. However, the majority of its graduates stays and practices in the Midwest. In big Midwestern legal markets such as Chicago, Minneapolis, and Indianapolis, a law degree from Iowa carries a good deal of weight. But the farther away from the epicenter in Iowa City, the fewer heads an Iowa degree will turn. My friend who applied to Iowa wanted to practice in his hometown of Los Angeles—or at least somewhere in California. He would have been just about clinically insane to have gone to Iowa. He would have had a stronger hand finding a job in L.A. going to a local school, even if it didn't rank as highly as Iowa in national rankings (especially if his performance at that local school was better than it might have been at Iowa). By going to a school in the area that you want to practice, you will have several advantages when it comes to finding a job: local law firms will recruit at your school; there will be a stronger alumni network; and you can be sure that people will have at least heard of your school and will likely be willing to hire (or at least consider) one of its graduates.

The golden rule should help you zero in on the right law school for you. But what do you do if you don't know where you want to live and work for the rest of your life? You might need a different book to help you here—such as a travel guide. The United States of America is so vast that you could go just about anywhere and make a good living as an attorney. When I was a kid I lived in Argentina, a country where about a quarter of the population lives in the capital city of Buenos Aires. Aspiring law students in Argentina don't have this dilemma because they know that if they want to study and practice law—or anything else for that matter—the best bet is to go to Buenos Aires.

Fortunately for Americans, there is good work to be found away from the big cities. Still, many aspiring law students have the impression that their best bet is to go to the big city legal markets, such as New York, Chicago, San Francisco, or Los Angeles. They figure that since these areas are densely populated, there will naturally be a big demand for attorneys, and plenty of job opportunities. It's true that these areas have big populations, and a lot of people need a lot of lawyers. But unfortunately, you're too late. That big demand for attorneys has been met and over-supplied many times over. It's common to hear non-lawyers say that there are too many lawyers in this country. While you might expect an attorney to be offended by this comment, lawyers are the first people to admit they are overabundant.

The major legal markets do offer plenty of work for attorneys, but the problem for the newly graduated law student is that finding a job in a major legal market is extraordinarily competitive. For example, say you want to become an attorney in Manhattan. Of course you do; everyone in the world wants to be a rich, bad-ass lawyer in Manhattan, wearing expensive suits and dating supermodels. I respect those with big aspirations, but try to be realistic. Suppose you decide to live and work in Manhattan and end up going to a decent but not spectacular law school in or around the City. Now, look what you're up against. You'll not only be competing with students from the outstanding local schools—NYU and Columbia—but also from *all* the Ivy League law schools *and* other top-tier powerhouses. The same goes for Chicago. You'll have graduates from the University of Chicago and Northwestern going after the same jobs as you, as well as from every top school in the Midwest—from Michigan to our old friend the University of Iowa.

Before moving to Florida, I considered staying in California and looking for a job in either L.A. or San Francisco. I quickly realized that all the top firms had plenty of job-hungry applicants, from more desirable schools like Stanford, UC–Berkeley, UCLA, and USC. (Not to mention a bunch of East Coast kids from Harvard and Yale wanting to take in some of that California sunshine.) I felt like a scrappy hyena waiting for the lions to finish eating the best meat and leave me with at least one morsel from what was left of the carcass.

I'm not saying you'll be unemployed if you go to a less reputable school. What I *am* saying is that in a competitive legal market, the best jobs tend to go to the students from the best schools. You can still get a good job with a decent salary, but keep in mind that life in the big cities is expensive. Your decent salary might not cut it like it would in a smaller town. You may have dreamed of living in Manhattan, wearing expensive suits, and dating supermodels; you might have to settle for living in Queens, wearing suits from Men's Wearhouse, and dating paralegals.

You may ask yourself, "But other than the big cities, where else is there to go?"

Well, why go anywhere? Why not stay where you are? I completely understand if someone has had it with life in their hometown, and feels that they *have* to leave and start a life somewhere else. After all, I used law school as an excuse to get the hell out of Indianapolis. I don't regret my decision to leave Indianapolis; I'm a happier person having done so. But again, from that responsible, career-oriented perspective, I would have been better off staying in Indianapolis. There's a cost to leaving any home town.

The Indiana University system has two good law schools: a great, top-tier one in Bloomington, and a respectable, second-tier one in Indianapolis. Had I gone to either one I would have saved a ton of money paying in-state tuition and down-to-Earth rent, as opposed to the steep private-school tuition and ridiculous rent I paid in California. More importantly, I would've had a *much* easier time finding a good job after graduation. I knew many people in Indianapolis, my parents had many semi-important friends, and my former boss was well connected within Indianapolis' legal, business, and political circles. As the saying goes, it's who you know that counts. Often, the most important factor for finding a job is to know the right people. As an attorney, one of the most marketable qualities is knowing—or getting to know—potential clients. Therefore, unless you absolutely hate where you live, the smart move might be to stay put. Starting your career in your hometown, or at least your home state, can often make the most practical sense. If you're comfortable where you are, why move?

I once met a law student who had a thick Southern accent. When I asked him where he was from, he told me he was from Alabama. (Not a surprising response, of course.) When I asked him where he went to law school, however, his answer shocked me. He told me he went to some small school I had never heard of in Cleveland, Ohio. I thought this to be incredibly strange.

I know Alabama isn't exactly the Garden of Eden, but I'll be darned if it isn't better than Cleveland. At least Alabama has good weather and some nice beaches on the Gulf of Mexico. I can understand if someone from Cleveland or from some nearby town might go to that law school. But I couldn't understand why someone from Alabama would choose to leave his family, friends, and familiar surroundings to go to *Cleveland*. Don't get me wrong, I can understand why he would want to leave Alabama, but of all the places in the country, how the Hell did he settle on Cleveland?

I thus politely asked him the obvious question: "Why did you decide to go *there?*" Surely, I thought, he must have a good explanation—maybe they offered him a generous scholarship, or maybe he had family in Cleveland.

"Well," he answered with his drawl, "they sent me a brochure in the mail, so I applied there and they accepted me." That must've been one hell of a brochure.

"So do you like Cleveland?" I asked him.

"Not really." Then, after a second thought, "It's alright."

If *you* decide to leave the comforts and privileges of your hometown or state, make sure you have a good reason for doing so. And whatever you do, don't leave your home to go someplace worse. If you have to move, you should move up.

4

WELCOME TO LAW SCHOOL

So you've made it through the application process. You were accepted, and you decided which law school to attend. Now, the real fun (or lack thereof) begins. Welcome to law school.

Law school is like a marathon, and you should approach it as such. At the big marathons, like the one in New York, Boston, or Chicago, thousands line up at the starting line. Runners of all ages and shapes voluntarily decide to endure a grueling 26.2-mile race. Nearly everyone at the starting line thinks they'll finish the course, but along the way, many quit. The ones who finish look exhausted but delighted, and as a reward for enduring such a task, they get a certificate saying they completed the marathon, and the right to tell people so.

Law school is the same; it just takes a hell of a lot longer than a marathon. Not to say that marathon runners have it easy, but at least while they're running they know that the race will be over in a few hours, and tomorrow they won't have to think about running ever again. A law student—reading his tenth case of the night, or sweating through the fourth essay in an exam—can't look forward to tomorrow, because tomorrow it starts all over again, and again the next day, and so on for three years.

To run a marathon, a runner must pace himself. If he starts off with a sprint, he'll be done after a few miles. He has to maintain a pace that he can handle for the entirety of the race. In order to finish law school successfully, a law student should pace himself in a similar way.

One of my good friends started law school with a full-on sprint. For the first few months, he studied all the time, he was enthusiastic about the material, and he constantly participated in class. When he had a midterm for one of his classes, he studied his ass off and got a really good grade. At this point, he started to get cocky. "Law school is easy," he gloated, "I'll get straight As."

Fast forward to second semester. My friend starts to feel a little burned out and stops studying so much. (This is just as everyone else, scared from their first exams, begins to really ratchet up their study habits.) He no longer participates in class, and often shows up unprepared. When I talk to him as final exams are coming up, he says to me, "Dude, I'm just going for Cs."

Fast-forward to second year. He stops going to class almost entirely. He performs poorly on exams and ends up on academic probation. He will have to repeat classes the next year, and it looks as if he will not graduate with his class.

Fast-forward to third year. He manages to keep his grades up a little higher and graduates, albeit at the bottom of the class. In the end, that midterm he took first semester of the first year turned out to be the highest grade he ever got in law school. It was all downhill from there.

My friend's problem was that he didn't pace himself. He started with a sprint and ran out of gas. While his experience was a little extreme, I noticed many other classmates who started off with enthusiasm and high aspirations, only to crawl across the finish line on graduation day. Try to keep a pace that you can maintain for three years, one semester at a time. Don't kill yourself at the beginning of the semester if it means your brain won't be fresh for exams in a few months. Don't give it all you have first semester if it means you'll be so sick of law school by second semester that you'll stop going to class. Keep a nice, steady pace. Law school is a marathon; don't be like my friend and run a 100-yard dash.

One other distinctive aspect about a marathon as a sporting event (sorry for beating this marathon metaphor to the ground) is that while thousands of runners participate, only a small percentage of the runners are actually competing to *win* the race. There are usually a handful of Kenyans who battle for first place. A few hundred serious runners who might have run cross-country in college would love to tell people they got 287th place at the Boston Marathon. Finally, there are a few thousand non-competitive runners, who might be men with boring jobs or women with three kids or [fill in the blank]. They want nothing more than to go back to the suburbs and tell their neighbors that they *did it.* They ran—and finished—a *marathon*. Every runner has his own goal and his own standard of success; it's a beautiful thing.

Law school is not like that. In law school, no matter what your personal goals are, everyone is in direct competition with every other student. The way the system is set up, success is not measured by how much you learn the law; it's measured by how much more you know about the law than the guy next to you. Law exams are graded on a curve. This means that your performance on an exam is based on how well you did as compared to your classmates. Then, when your grades come out, you don't get to decide for yourself how well you did. The Registrar compiles your grades, compares them to everyone else's grades, and the results are revealed in the class rankings. To know exactly how good about yourself you should feel, you get a little percentage number assigned to your name that shows you—and anyone who asks, including recruiters—how much better or worse you are than everyone else.

For example, if your class rank is in the top 10%, you're like one of those bad-ass Kenyan runners. If you rank within the top 10%–25%, you're like one of those serious runners who ran cross-country in college. And if you rank anywhere below the top 25%...sorry, you're one among the masses from the suburbs who walk halfway and are glad to cross the marathon off their life's to-do list.

One of my good friends from high school went to law school a year before I did. After his first year was over, I asked him how he had done. He became noticeably upset and told me he hadn't done very well. I asked him what his GPA was and he told me it was a 3.2.

"What are you talking about?" I jumped at him, "a 3.2 isn't bad at all."

He morosely explained to me: "It's not like college. In law school the only thing that matters is your class rank. And with my grades, I'm only at the top 40% of the class."

"That's not that bad," I tried to console him.

"You wouldn't think so," he replied, "but it kind of *is.*"

If you don't like the competitive nature of law school, you can voice your complaint to the American Bar Association. During law school, I heard many of my professors confess that they didn't like having to curve exams and that they would like to give out more As and Bs. But professors have strict orders from the administration, who in turn have strict orders from the ABA to curve everything and rank everyone. Some of the top law schools in the country, such as UC–Berkley's Boalt School of Law, or Yale Law School are trying to make some much-needed changes to the grading system, to make it less cutthroat and competitive, and more focused on, well, legal education. This is easier for schools like UC–Berkley or Yale to do because of their impeccable reputations. Lesser-known law schools have to be careful to keep their lips closely glued to the ABA's posterior, and must unquestioningly do everything it asks of them. Otherwise, the ABA could put them on probation, or take away their accreditation. Being unaccredited is the worst possible fate for a law school—worse than being in *U.S. News'* fourth tier, by far. An unaccredited law school might as well be an air-conditioning repair school.

So why does law school have to be so competitive? Why do there have to be curved exams and class ranks? Again, it's to help law firms with their hiring process. By having a class rank, the work load for law firm recruiters is considerably cut down. This way, they don't have to sort through millions of résumés and cover letters.

When recruiters come to law schools looking for potential associates, they don't come with open arms like the Statue of Liberty, reciting: "Give me your tired, your poor, your huddled masses yearning to practice law." They come with an "I'm busy, don't waste my time" attitude and say, "Send me the top 10% of your second-year class, and I might offer them jobs."

The better the law firm, the more limited the percentage of students they'll consider. The best big law firms will only interview applicants from the top 5% to 10% of a class. The medium sized firms might consider applicants as low as the top 25%. The other 75% of the class will be lucky to work for a small firm or solo practitioner for $15 to $30 an hour. While $30 an hour used to sound pretty good to me, after hearing what the summer associates at the big firms can make, it seemed like slave wages. Of course, this system is relative to the caliber of the law school you attend. If you are at the top 40% of your Harvard class, you'll still probably get a better job than someone at the top 10% of a second-tier school.

The competitive nature of law school does weird and dangerous things to law students. Even those who may have been pretty mellow before—wishing everybody well and minding their own business—become ultra-competitive fanatics and will not hesitate to do a victory dance if they hear a classmate got a C on an exam. Attorneys have a reputation for being cold-hearted, only caring about themselves and their personal success. While this isn't entirely true, there are plenty of assholes practicing law out there. Many of these cold-hearted attorneys were not born this way; they are the product of the ultra-competitive, dog-eat-dog law school system.

From the first day of law school, students are pitted against each other in direct competition. Your classmates—with whom you're supposed to become friends and future colleagues—are the ones who eventually, if indirectly, determine your success. If your best friend does better than you, it means that you are one slot lower in the class rank thanks to him. Virtues like loyalty and that chivalrous *may the best man win* attitude are the first to go out the window. Fair play flies out the window shortly thereafter.

After three years in such an environment, a person learns to look out for himself and nobody else. When a newly graduated, freshly certified attorney is let loose, he probably knows very little about how the legal profession actually works. But he's sure as hell certain about one thing: the only thing that matters is winning. If ethical and moral barriers have to be sidestepped in order to win, so be it.

Law schools act as if they're horrified by the lack of ethics within the legal profession. They make students take mandatory legal ethics courses, and some make students participate in mandatory pro-bono work. Interestingly, even the legal ethics courses are curved. So at exam time, you have a class full of future attorneys wishing the guy next to him won't know anything about ethics. When the grades come out, the select few students who get an A can look at all their classmates with certainty and say: "That's right, bitch. I'm more ethical than you."

There's an academy in Fort Benning, Georgia officially called the Western Hemisphere Institute for Security Cooperation, but affectionately known as the School of the Americas. The academy, operated by the United States military, has historically been like West Point for Latin American military personnel who aspire to one day return to their home countries and use their training to stage a *coup d'etat* and become rogue, totalitarian dictators. Such well-recognized alumni include Panama's Manuel Noriega and Chile's Augusto Pinochet.

Just as a good law school would, the School of the Americas plays innocent whenever one of its graduates does something evil. And just as law schools require students to take a course in professional ethics, the School of the Americas now has mandatory human rights courses as part of their curriculum. But I still get the impression that whenever a Latin American general overthrows a democratically elected president, or whenever a lawyer tampers with some evidence, both School of the Americas or law school officials probably react the same way. They might say, *"Oops,"* closely followed by a more silent, "...I'll be damned if we didn't teach him well."

The sad part is that coming into law school, law students tend to be very nice people. However, more than nice, they tend to be highly self-driven and determined to succeed. For the most part, law students are those kids who always got good grades in high school and college. Since law school is so demanding and difficult to get into, the only ones who end up having the grades or the determination to get through it are the ones who stayed in their dorms to study during college, while everyone else was out partying.

This is probably a good thing. Otherwise, you might have people going to law school on a whim after watching *A Few Good Men* on the *USA Network* one night and feeling inspired. Or worse, law schools might fill up with those meatheads who like to argue when they're drunk. (Convincing your fraternity brothers that Bud Light has funnier commercials than Miller Lite is probably not sufficiently predictive of a successful career in the law).

Coming into law school, most students are used to getting good grades and feeling successful. The difference is that in college—and high school before that—they were in nearly complete control of how well they did. They knew that if they studied hard and put forth an adequate effort, getting an A was plausible. For some, merely paying attention was enough for the A. In law school, all of a sudden they're no longer in control. Studying hard is no longer enough. Now, it's all about studying harder than the next guy. Many students remain confident and think, "That's okay; I always got better grades than everyone else in college." That may be true. But think about it...in law school *everyone* got the best grades in college. Now you're picking on people your own size. You're in direct competition with a bunch of nerds just like yourself.

So from day one, every law student appears to be two things: stressed out and suspicious. Sure, externally everyone seems nice and polite, but on the inside, everyone is measuring everyone else up. When you first meet a classmate and talk to him, you may notice he's a little bit distracted from the actual conversation. That's because he's trying to determine—by what you're saying and by what he knows about you—just how smart you are, and what kind of threat you present to him. For example, if you went to an Ivy League school for undergrad, people will assume you're a contender. Unless you say something retarded in class one day, you're pretty safe. If you went to a college that nobody's heard of, you'd better have some other tricks up your sleeve.

One of my friends in law school had the misfortune of being a big, fat, beer-guzzling, football-obsessed fraternity guy from a state university in the Midwest. Nobody took him seriously. He was just the guy who was fun to hang out with while eating pizza and watching ESPN. Everything changed when some valuable information was leaked. It turned out that, back in high school, this supposed meathead had been the Illinois State Chess Champion two years in a row. I don't even know if it was true or not, but overnight he went from being John Belushi to Bobby Fisher. All of a sudden, he was some sort of genius that everyone should keep an eye on.

My first year of law school, I lived in an apartment complex that housed only first-year law students. Living there was exhausting; it was like *Melrose Place*...but with ugly people, really boring plot lines, and far too little sex. Everyone was perpetually concerned with what everyone else was doing. People would look up at their neighbors' windows to see who was studying, and for how long.

Comments would be made behind people's backs, such as: "Today in class, Professor Such-and-So asked [random student's name] a question and he didn't know the answer *at all!*" It was pathetic.

By nature, I'm pretty laid-back, so I tried not to take part. I hadn't come to law school to stress out about getting good grades, much less to stress out about *others'* grades. Hell, I could've stressed out in Indiana; I had come to California to have a good time. I studied a fair amount, but only as much as I felt was necessary. The rest of the time, I hung out with friends, I went to the beach, I went *out* at night, I took weekend trips, and did all the things I normally liked to do, regardless of whether I was a first-year law student. Eventually, I started to notice that people had been keeping tabs on me. Without even knowing it, I developed a reputation as a slacker who never studied—and thus wasn't a threat to anyone.

I noticed that people spoke to me differently than they had at the beginning of the year. Before, I would get the requisite investigatory questions such as: "Where'd you go to college?" "What was your major?" Little facts that need to be known to determine someone's potential. Kind of like high school. Pathetic, but true. After a while, however, other students would approach me with ease and say stupid little comments like, "Wow, you're pretty tan. Were you at the beach *again* this weekend?"

"Yeah you pale bastard," I wanted to respond. "Of course I went to the beach. Why the hell wouldn't I?"

Or if someone saw me at the library, he might jokingly say: "Hey, is this your first time in here?"

"Yeah, it is," I had to bite my lip to keep from saying. "And it's probably the last, if I have to run in to douche-bags like you here."

But, like I mentioned, I'm a laid-back guy, so I just smiled and made pleasant small talk.

Everything changed once first semester exams came around. Most of our first year classes lasted the whole year, so most of the exams were only midterms. The big one, however, was Criminal Law. This class was only a semester long, so this was the only exam that determined the entire final grade. This was our first exam, and the most important one of the semester. I reached far up into, well, somewhere, and pulled out a big, fat A.

Me—the slacker who spent more time at the beach than the library—had gotten one of the select few As out of the entire first-year class.

Word got out that I had gotten an A. (In other words, I told everyone I knew.) I've enjoyed few joys as great as watching the reactions on their faces when I told them I had set the curve. People were shocked. All of a sudden, my reputation changed. While some sore losers insisted that I had gotten lucky, others began to see me as some sort of mysterious genius who didn't need to study and could still get better grades than anyone. I was their worst nightmare. Though grossly inaccurate, this reputation followed me for the remainder of my three years. In law school, an A can go a very, very long way.

5

CLASS IS IN SESSION

During my third year of law school, I suffered a pretty serious head injury while snowboarding in Lake Tahoe, resulting in an operation to have blood drained out of my skull. Everything went well until I was told that my medical bills totaled fifty-four thousand dollars. I couldn't believe it. "That's how much a year and a half of law school costs!"

"Oh well," I thought, "at least I'm healthy, and you can't really put a price on your health."

No, you can't put a price on your health. But apparently, if you're a hospital's billing department, you can put a price on everything else. When I looked at the detailed bill, they had charged me for everything but the individual breaths I took. Every time the nurse offered me morphine and I said yes, it was about $200. Every time the nurse dumped a pan of my urine into the toilet, it was about $150. Paying $54,000 to be alive—and with no significant brain damage—sounds reasonable; paying $300 to have a nurse yank a catheter out of your penis is just painful.

Similarly, when you take a step back and look at law school, the price of tuition doesn't seem entirely outrageous. I went to a private school where tuition cost around $30,000 a year. So if someone were to ask me how much my law degree cost me, I could give them a basic figure of $90,000. (If you go to a state school, prices are more reasonable: usually around $10,000–$15,000 per year, for a total of $30,000–$45,000. Lower, but still far from cheap). Upon first hearing such a high figure, most become shocked. When they then take into account how much money an attorney can make throughout his career, that $90,000 is probably a reasonable investment. That's the macro perspective.

If you look with a magnifying glass and analyze a law school bill from a micro perspective, however, you might start to wonder whether you're spending your money wisely. Tuition is not determined by semester or academic year, but by units. At a private law school, one unit can cost around $1,500, and most classes are made up of three units, so a single class can cost $4,500. If you forget for a minute that you're paying for a big shiny *Juris Doctor,* and look at each class as an individual experience that's costing you $4,500, you might start to feel like you're getting ripped off.

Maybe you'll have a few classes that interest you, where the professor is exceptional, and in the end, you feel that you got a lot out of the experience. In such occasions, maybe that $4,500 is justified. But for every class like that one, I took at least three that bored me out of my mind and made me feel that the professor should've been paying me to sit there and humor him. Nevertheless, those classes still cost the same standard rate of $4,500 a pop.

To put it into perspective with other expenditures, I bought my first car—which I drove for six years and thousands of miles all over the United States—for $3,500. Sure, I bought it used, and I admit there was an occasion when I parked it on Rodeo Drive in Beverly Hills and I felt like an entirely inadequate human being. But considering the use I got out of that car, that $3,500 might have been the best money I ever spent. You have to differentiate between cost and value. The personal value that car had for me, making me mobile for so many years and miles, far exceeded its $3,500 cost. On the other hand, the personal value my obscenely boring Contracts class had for me pales in comparison to its ridiculous cost. Since it was two semesters long, my Contracts class cost me $9,000 (that's about as much as I paid for my entire Bachelor's Degree). In that course, I learned about unconscionable contracts, and I can't think of a better example of one than my being duped into paying $9,000 to sit in such a terrible year-long class.

But, if you're already set on going through with this crazy law school idea, then there's no point in talking about cost. As long as the number of law school applicants keeps rising, the law schools can charge whatever they want. The only thing you can do to fight it is not go to law school. So ignore your economic conscience and look at law school costs as one giant expenditure; one giant investment. This way it will be much easier to stomach.

ATTENDANCE

When I had my snowboarding accident and surgery, I missed three weeks of class. You would think that missing so much class might force me to repeat the semester. However, one of the few beauties of law school is that class attendance is rarely mandatory. (It is to the ABA, and thus that's the official policy, but it's not in the sense of yelling "Present!" as when a teacher would call roll at the beginning of class.) It's also sometimes unnecessary.

At my law school, on the first semester of the first year, attendance *was* mandatory. Everyone had to sign next to their printed name on an attendance sheet posted on the wall. Many people still skipped class and simply had friends forge their signatures for them. The Student Records Office checked the lists of names, but there were so many students and so many classes, they simply kept an eye out for a blank slot next to someone's name. Inspecting the accuracy of each signature would have taken them forever. After the first semester, the attendance requirement seemed to be lifted, and for the next two and a half years, only two or three of my professors ever took attendance.

Now, just because you're not required to go to class doesn't mean you shouldn't go. After all, as we discussed earlier, you're paying a lot of money to be there. Therefore, I developed two personal "golden rules for class attendance." The first one:

Don't skip class if the professor will notice that you're missing. For just about every class you take in law school, your grade will be based almost entirely on your performance on the final exam. However, professors are allowed to allot a limited amount of points for participation. You can be pretty certain that you'll get a bad participation grade if your professor is aware that you skip his class every day. If you're confident that you'll do well enough in the exam to sacrifice your participation points, go ahead and do whatever you want. But my advice is not to get too cocky. Take all the points you can get.

Most law school classes, especially the required ones, are crowded. Depending on the size of your law school, any required classes —or the ones for subjects that are tested on the Bar Exam—will probably have between 50 and 125 students. With that many students in a room, the professor won't notice that you're missing unless you normally sit under his nose in the front row, or look like the Elephant Man.

On the other hand, some classes, especially the more obscure elective courses, will have as few as 10–15 students, making it harder to skip without the professor noticing. I attended my smaller classes because: (a) I wanted to remain in the professor's good side; and (b) I would feel bad if a few other students might skip that day and the professor would have to give his lecture, awkwardly, to five students.

Another situation where a professor might notice that you're missing is if he calls on you and you're not there. Believe me; you don't want a professor calling out your name a couple of times only to realize you're not present. When this happens, professors tend to get frustrated because it halts class, and a little embarrassed because of the complete silence. The worst is when a professor calls three or four names in a row and *no one* is there. In these cases, professors tend to get pissed off, and if they didn't take attendance before, they might very well start.

My little trick for courses in which the professor called on people at random was that I tried to never skip two classes in a row. Oftentimes, if a professor calls on someone who isn't there, he'll try him again the next time. If that student isn't there the second time around, the professor will assume he never goes to class. But if he's present the second time, the professor may just assume he had a good reason for missing class on the first occasion. Another option is to keep a few friends in your classes so they can tell you when the professor happens to call your name. (Just make sure your friends go to class.)

After you apply the first golden rule and you determine that you can skip class safely without the professor noticing, you can apply the second golden rule:

Go to class if you think that it's worth your while and it's the best use of your time. The main objective of law school is to learn the law, and each course is designed to help you learn about a certain area of law. Ideally, every class would be worth your while and would be useful for you to learn what you need to know. Most classes achieve this objective. However, on some occasions, a professor will not be as competent as you would like him to be, and going to that class is simply not worth your time.

Though some professors may act like it, they're not the only ones who know the law, and they aren't the only ones who can teach it to you. For most classes, especially in the required Bar subjects, you can learn everything you need to know for the exam without ever stepping foot inside the classroom. You can probably learn everything by reading your textbook, as well as some of the various available commercial outlines.

Still, even if you don't think you need to attend a particular class, it might be worth your while to go. Professors can clarify certain points that might be confusing if you just read about them in a book, and participating in discussions can help you grasp a better understanding of an issue. Perhaps most importantly, by going to class you can get a feel for what issues your professor considers to be most important. This way, you'll have a pretty good idea of what kind of questions he'll ask in the exam.

If you're absolutely certain that going to a particular class is not worth your while, and every time you go to that class you feel like you just wasted an hour and a half of your life, then it's probably in your best interest to skip. However, skipping a class shouldn't be an excuse to sleep in late, watch TV, or play video games. If you skip class, maximize that time. Make good use of it. You could, for example, use that hour and a half to study, or look for a summer job.

When I took Constitutional Law, I had the misfortune of having a terrible professor. After going to class for the first few weeks, I finally decided that attendance was not worth my while, and my time could be better spent doing something else. However, I realized that Constitutional Law was an important course that had to be taken seriously; not only for my grade, but because it's a foundational course. Therefore, I decided that every time my class met, instead of attending, I would dedicate that time to studying Constitutional Law. This way, instead of wasting two hours in class, I maximized my time and *actually learned* Constitutional Law.

I know a lawyer who, for his last two years as a law student, barely attended any of the classes in which he was enrolled; he would simply show up for the exam at the end of the semester. This doesn't mean that he took a two-year vacation, though I'm sure he would've loved to. On the contrary, he spent those two years working *full-time* as a clerk at a law firm. He received a terrific education with invaluable hands-on experience, and made a decent salary that paid for his tuition. It was a much better use of his time than sitting in on boring lectures. He studied, took the exams with all the other students, and got good grades. By the time he graduated, he had two years of work experience and as good a grasp of the law—if not a better one—as any of his classmates.

Of course, if you choose to do something like that, you have to do it *very carefully,* very much under the radar. No law school offers such leniency that would allow you to officially skip your classes and work a full-time job. No matter how good your persuasion skills may be, I doubt any law student could ever convince his Dean of Students to give him a two-year hall pass. However, if you are *extremely* dedicated and self-motivated (as you really *do* have to learn the law, either way, and if you skip class you have to, in essence, teach yourself), working at a law firm in lieu of going to class might not only be possible, it might also be beneficial. But you didn't read that here.

Decide for yourself. If you have better things to do than sitting in on a class that isn't worth your while, then don't. You don't need anyone's permission. But don't waste that time.

CASES

When I was first in law school, I expected classes to pretty much resemble my undergraduate classes. I was wrong. Law school classes have a unique method and structure that is quite different from any other academic classes you have taken. With a few minor differences here and there, just about every class in law school is run in the same way. While some professors tend to be more innovative than others, most run their classes the same way, year after year. And classes are run the same way as when law professors were law students. (The main difference is that students now take notes on laptops rather than notebooks.)

Law school classes focus almost entirely on court cases. Most of the time, you will read and discuss appellate decisions written by appellate judges or Supreme Court justices. When studying a common law legal system such as the American one, attention must be paid to individual, ground-breaking case decisions and their reasoning. For three years, taking five or so courses per semester, you'll read and discuss *hundreds* of cases. After a while, law school becomes a mental juggling act, trying to remember which case was in which subject, what happened, who sued whom, and for what.

Reading cases is supposed to train a law student to become familiar with legal language and the structure of court decisions. After all, new attorneys will scan more cases in a week than a law student tries to in a year. It helps to be able to understand just what the Hell the judge is talking about.

When I was an English major in college I had to read Chaucer's *Canterbury Tales* in the original Middle English. For those of you who haven't read it—or were lucky enough to read the modern English translation—the Middle English version reads kind of like German mixed with gibberish. Still, I can promise you that I had an easier time deciphering what Chaucer was saying than what some of the country's finest justices had to say about such common legal concepts as *Promissory Estoppel.*

The frustrating thing is that the law isn't really that complicated. It's just made to sound and seem complicated by the judges who write case decisions and the professors who teach them. For example, despite the overcomplicated name it was given, the concept of *promissory estoppel* is actually a simple, common-sense idea. Essentially, if you tell someone you're going to do something for him, and he's relying on you to do it, a court can force you to do what you were supposed to, even if there was no written contract.

Okay, you might have to read that sentence a second time. And, yes, there are a few intricacies to be considered. The point is that the concept of *promissory estoppel* can be summed up neatly with a clear and concise explanation. There's really no need to dedicate two weeks and five long, complicated cases to it. That only makes things *more* tedious and confusing.

There's a simpler and more efficient way to teach someone the concept of *promissory estoppel*—or any legal concept for that matter. But law professors aren't charged with simplicity and efficiency. For something that could be explained in one paragraph and in about five minutes, they assign a fifteen page case and spend two hours discussing it. Law students end up confused, stressed out, and doing way more work than is necessary.

COMMERCIAL OUTLINES

From somewhere in the heavens, God saw how law professors were making life miserable for law students, and he didn't like it. So, while on the first day he created light, on a day just as important for law students everywhere, he created commercial outlines.

Some don't believe in commercial outlines, or supplements, and look down on students who use them. They consider it akin to a professional athlete using steroids to get an advantage over his competitors. If anything, students using supplements is more like athletes drinking Gatorade. Sure, you can just drink water, but Gatorade tastes better and has electrolytes to help replenish your body's needs during and after a workout. Sure, you can just read the textbook and listen to your professor, but commercial outlines have everything you need to know in short, easy-to-digest gulps.

If you consider the use of supplements to be immoral, don't use them. I suppose I could learn to admire that kind of stubborn work ethic. But don't complain when your classmates finish studying two hours before you and can go to bed, while they manage to learn just as much as you. Besides, it's not as if supplements are illegal. The bookstore at your law school will sell them right next to your required textbooks. Bookstores make a lot of money off of these supplements, so they'll not likely stop selling them any time soon.

But while they're not forbidden, many professors don't like to see their students using them. So if you bring them to class, for goodness sake don't wave them in front of your professor's face or quote freely from them during class. And whatever you do, don't ever tell your professor that what he's saying is contradictory to what your commercial outline says.

There are two kinds of supplements: case summaries and legal outlines. Do yourself a favor and get one of each.

Case Summaries. Case summaries do the hard work of a case for you. Instead of trudging through five pages of inarticulate legalese, you get everything meaningful you need to know in about a page. If you're still too lazy to read one page, don't worry. At the top of the page, in bold letters, there will be one sentence describing the facts of the case and one sentence telling you the ruling. If you're too lazy to read two sentences, then please do your professors, classmates, and future clients a favor: Just drop out.

There are several publishers of case summaries. My favorites are the *High Court* series as the others can be less substantial; but judge for yourself. With summaries you'll get the main gist of a case. If a professor calls on you to talk about that case, that's all you'll be able to tell him, the main gist. The *High Court* ones tend to include enough information to make it sound as if you actually read the case. If anything, you'll sound as if a few things (understandably) slipped your mind.

Let me warn you though: case summaries are addicting. I discovered them about midway through my first semester of law school and bought one for each of my classes. At first, I told myself I would still read the case decisions, just referring to the case summaries if I didn't understand something. That lasted about an hour. As Churchill said, why stand when you can sit? There was no need to read the entire decisions when I could get just as much out of a case summary. In fact, I often got *more* out of reading the summaries. Case decisions are so long and boring that my mind always started to wander once I hit the second page. At about the sixth page, I would catch myself and say, "Wait a minute. What did I just read?"

Those case summaries made first year bearable. I was hooked on them. When second year came around, it turned out that a couple of my classes didn't have case summaries available. (Case summaries are made to match the most widely used textbooks for the most widely taken courses. If you take an obscure elective course, or your professor chooses an unpopular textbook, you're out of luck.)

Here I was, having to read entire case decisions again. I was out of practice. My mind had gotten lazy and it was hard for me to get through a single case. It's like when people start using reading glasses. At first, they can see okay without them, but once they wear them for a while and get accustomed to them, there's no going back.

Legal Outlines. The second type of supplement, and the one that is most widely used, is the legal outline. Legal outlines are *very* handy books that break down an area of law into its core elements. They take everything that your professor talks about in class, peel away all the unnecessary layers, and give you the information you need in short, black-letter sentences.

It's like the difference between watching CNN and its sister channel, Headline News. With CNN, you get in-depth looks at individual news stories. They show live press conference footage and interview experts on both sides of the spectrum. If you watch for fifteen minutes, you'll come away knowing a lot about one or two news stories. On the other hand, Headline News throws out news stories like a black-jack dealer tossing out cards. If you watch for fifteen minutes, you'll know a little bit about every major news story in the country. You may not get all the little details, but you'll know enough not to seem ignorant at the water cooler.

Legal outlines are perfect for lazy, cheap, or physically weak law students. They're short and easy to read, cost about one-third of the price of a textbook, and weigh about 15 pounds less. If you're satisfied with just the general information and the black-letter-law of a subject, then these outlines will suit you fine. If you want more details and you enjoy being a spectator in the law's back-and-forth tennis matches between judges who keep contradicting each other, then stick with your case book and listen to your professor.

However, just because you're a more involved and enthusiastic law student doesn't mean you should disregard legal outlines; they could still be a helpful study tool for you. Legal outlines are perfect for refreshing your memory. No matter how good a grasp you may have on an issue while you're studying it, after a few weeks pass, it will seem as vague as a childhood memory. This is especially true when you're juggling five different courses that will occasionally resemble each other and eventually confuse the Hell out of you. Before you know it, you'll be applying tort law to a criminal case and vice versa. When you forget something, or are confused by it, simply open your legal outline to the index, find what you're looking for, and *voilà!* After a few short passages, your mind is refreshed and your confusion subsides.

There are many legal outline series. In my opinion, the best ones are the *Gilbert* outlines, followed by *Emmanuel*. I loved the *Gilbert* outlines and whenever there was one available for my class I would automatically buy it. The problem with the *Gilbert* outlines though, is that they have them only for the core classes. *Emmanuel* has a zillion outlines and they cover almost every course you'll take, with the exception of the most obscure elective subjects. When *Gilbert* wasn't available for a class, I would go with *Emmanuel*.

The main difference between the two is that the *Gilbert* outlines tend to be more concise, while the *Emmanuel* ones are packed with information. Some people like that about them and get scared by *Gilbert's* more minimalist approach. For example, one of my good friends was a big information nerd; he liked to know everything about a certain issue. For that reason, he preferred the *Emmanuel* outlines. To me that seems to defeat the purpose of an outline: to break a subject down to its core elements. But that's the joy of both: you choose whichever works better for you.

The most useful outlines tend to be those written by the author of your textbook. (Publishers try to get the professors who write the major casebooks to write or at least supervise the outlines.) If you're lucky enough to find such an outline, you know it will match your casebook—and course syllabus—perfectly. Professors tend to structure classes around the case book they choose, so an outline written by the author of your textbook will pretty much be a concise summary of your entire course.

My first year, I was lucky enough to have outlines for both my Criminal Law and Property classes that were written by the authors of the casebooks. They were extremely helpful. I used them until the pages fell off and managed to get an A in Criminal Law and a B+ in Property. Without the aid of these supplements, I would have had to study much harder, for a much longer time, and I'm sure I would not have done as well.

THE SOCRATIC METHOD

When I was in college, I knew a girl who was deathly afraid of public speaking. She sounded articulate and perfectly normal when she spoke privately to only one or two others, but whenever she had to address a crowd larger than about five, she would develop an atrocious speech impediment. She would talk as if her tongue was too big and heavy for her mouth, lisp, and omit entire, crucial syllables when saying certain words. This caused her so much grief that she went out of her way to never take a class if she would have to give a presentation. She even changed her major because the one she had originally chosen required that she take a Speech and Communications class.

I didn't keep in touch with her after graduation, but the last time I talked to her, she told me she planned on going to law school. If indeed she ended up going to law school, my guess is that she probably dropped out soon thereafter. I'm guessing that after the first or second time a professor singled her out to answer his questions in front of about eighty of her classmates, she probably realized law school would be just too painful. That's too bad, as she was very intelligent and otherwise perfectly qualified.

Law professors love to put their students on the spot and ask them questions, even (and sometimes especially) if they don't raise their hands. They call this the Socratic Method. I call it a pain in the ass. In Ancient Greece, the great philosopher, Socrates, would educate his students by engaging in a dialogue with them, asking them questions and guiding them through their answers. If a student's answer was wrong, Socrates would prefer that the student figure out the flaw for himself. Through cooperative thinking, the pupil would eventually be enlightened and arrive at a proper conclusion. This way, instead of being *told* something and accepting it, a student would have to fully think about a concept, thus gaining a fuller understanding of it. Most law professors use this method, to some extent at least. Few professors actually lecture; they call on students and by asking them a series of questions, they guide the class through a particular concept or issue.

Theoretically, the Socratic Method has merit. If used correctly it can be an effective pedagogical tool. However, in a law school setting, it's often more problematic than helpful. First, most law school classes are too big for the Socratic Method to be effective. History tells us that the Socratic Method worked wonders for Socrates' star pupil, Plato. But you never hear anything about Plato's classmates. That's because while Plato was fumbling his thoughts around, pretty much thinking out loud, he was getting all-star tutelage, but everyone else was probably either bored or confused. That's the thing about the Socratic Method: it's helpful to the student who is being asked the questions, but not so much to everyone else in the class.

Oxford, Harvard's older English cousin, has a traditional tutorial method in which a student prepares an essay and then presents it and discusses it individually in a private session with his professor. In this one-on-one setting (or in very small groups of fewer than a dozen), the Socratic Method works very well indeed. Talk with anyone who's gone to Oxford or another school with a tutorial approach and you'll instantly see the difference. In law school, a professor discusses an issue with an individual student, while 75 other students watch. This not only causes the individual student to become extremely nervous and self-conscious, it provides a sub-par educational experience for the 75 spectator students. Don't worry—or actually, *do* worry—professors eventually get to everybody. But every time, it's the same thing, just with a different student. One student benefits, while 75 are left out.

It is frustrating. You have a professor who is extremely knowledgeable in his field and knows just about everything there is to know, but instead of telling the class something, he tries to pry it out of a poor, ignorant student. Oftentimes, the student is either unprepared, or just flat-out ignorant, so it takes the professor up to a half-hour to get the most basic correct answer. By the time the ignorant student is enlightened, everyone else has lost interest, stops paying attention, and turns their attention to the internet on their laptops.

Another frustrating example is when the student wanders (which is often). A professor asks an ignorant student a question that he doesn't know. In order not to seem clueless, the student gives a wrong answer with a great deal of conviction, so (he hopes) it *sounds* as if it is correct. Everyone in the class, convinced by his conviction, types the wrong answer into their notes. It usually takes the professor a few minutes to get the ignorant student to admit that he was wrong and another few minutes to guide him toward the right answer. By this point, the rest of the class has stopped paying attention. Half the class has the wrong answer typed and saved into their notes; the other half was smart enough to delete the wrong answer from their notes, but didn't bother to get the right one.

The other major complaint with the use of the Socratic Method is the obvious one: getting called on sucks, especially when you don't know the answer. The best—and perhaps the only—way to avoid being called on in years two and three is by taking classes taught by professors who won't call on you.

There are three kinds of law professor: the ones who only call on volunteers, the ones who call on students at random, and the ones who follow a pattern for calling on students.

Professors Who Call on Volunteers. The professors who only call on volunteers are the angels of law school. They are a witnessed miracle short of being canonized. They are kind enough to only call on people who want to be called on. They ask a question, and the first student to raise his hand gets to answer it. The atmosphere in these classes is much more relaxed, and the students tend to smile more.

However, sometimes the atmosphere gets a little too relaxed. If people know they won't be called on, they tend not to prepare as much for class. After the first few weeks, you might say, "I'll just skim this case; it's not like he's going to call on me," and by the end of the semester, you'll probably stop doing the reading entirely. That would be fine, except that all of your classmates end up doing the same thing, and after a certain point, there are only four or five loudmouths who consistently raise their hands and monopolize the class.

Eventually, the inevitable happens: the professor asks a question and nobody raises a hand. These are awkward moments. If too many of these moments occur, the angels lose their haloes. If he runs out of volunteers, a professor will feel forced to call on someone.

Professors Who Call at Random. While the professors who call on volunteers are the angels of law school, the ones who call on people at random are the demons. These are the most stressful and uncomfortable classes to be a part of. You can't just sit there, relax, and take in the information, because there is always a part of you that worries about getting called on.

I happen not to have a problem with public speaking, and I even enjoy giving an occasional presentation. While I'm no Martin

Luther King, I can usually get through a speech without making a complete moron of myself. This is true as long as I know in advance that I'm going to be speaking and there is enough time to prepare what I'm going to say. When you have a professor randomly call on you, you have neither of those luxuries. You'll be sitting in class, daydreaming, when all of a sudden you hear your name called. Up to that point, the professor probably said about 5,000 words and not one of them caught your attention. But no matter how far off your mind ever trails, you always register your name being called.

When this happens, everyone has a pretty similar reaction. They quickly raise their heads, sit up straight, do a little cough to clear their throats, and look directly at their textbooks. For some reason, everyone has the instinct to look at their textbook. A professor could ask a student for his mother's maiden name and he will look at his textbook for the answer. It's a type of defense mechanism for law students when they're caught off guard, or when they have no earthly idea what the answer might be. It gives them a few seconds to compose themselves and figure out what to say next. They're not actually reading any of the words in the book; they might as well be looking at a porn magazine. Looking at the textbook just beats staring dumb-faced at the professor.

If you do the reading for a class and pay attention, you should have little to worry about. Other than a few sadistic exceptions, professors aren't out to stump students. They usually have a destination in mind of where they want a lecture to go, and they'll ask the questions necessary to get there. So if you're prepared for class—unless you're like my friend with the public speaking anxiety and speech impediment—you'll be fine.

Actually, the one good thing about having a professor who calls at random is that it really *forces* you to study. Fear of looking like an idiot in front of your classmates is a great motivator. Still, there will be times when a professor catches you off-guard. For some reason or other you'll show up unprepared for class and get called on. You might try to play the odds and say, "I can skip the reading for today. Out of 80 students, there's no way he'll call on me." You might get away with this a few times, but sooner or later, the house is bound to win, no matter the odds.

This is when a law student's true colors shine. Anyone can answer a question about a case if he has read it. But to hold your own when you're put on the spot and you don't know the answer— that takes real tact. This will be one of the more valuable skills you will learn in law school. It's sort of like those commercials that try to get volunteers to join the Marines or the Army. They claim that after they finish serving, ex-Marines are able to perform under pressure and can confront any problem head-on. Law schools should advertise in a similar manner: after three years of law school, you'll be able to bullshit your way out of anything.

That's basically all you can do when a professor calls on you and you're not prepared. You can bullshit or you can pass. To be able to bullshit well is an art form. Some people are naturally gifted at it; others have to learn it and practice. But one thing is certain: to be a successful law student—and more importantly, to be a successful attorney—you have to be a good bullshitter.

For example, one of my law school friends was an absolute bullshit artist. He could talk around in circles and convince everyone— including the professor—that he knew what he was talking about, when in reality, he was clueless. We had a difficult class together, and on the few occasions when he was called on, he gave what sounded like perfectly good answers. I had fallen behind in the class, so I took a weekend to get caught up and try to figure out the material. I had a question about something, so I figured I would ask my friend since he seemed so well-versed in the subject. I asked him my question and he confessed, "Dude, I have no idea what's going on in that class. I'm completely lost." I couldn't believe it.

"But how do you always have a good answer when the professor calls on you?"

He was a little surprised and proud to have fooled me, "Are you kidding? I talk entirely out of my ass. I thought it was obvious."

I'm not as fortunate or naturally skilled to be able to bullshit as well as my friend. Don't get me wrong, in the right circumstances I can be pretty convincing about something I know little about. But I have to be at least *somewhat* knowledgeable about something before I can speak convincingly about it. My friend, on the other hand, could give you a sermon about a particular case decision having never read past the first sentence.

So my golden rule for faking it: *If you have enough of an idea about the case, then try to answer the question. If you have no idea, just pass.* It's like the advice you would get before taking the SATs, where you would lose points for guessing incorrectly on multiple-choice questions: if you have *some* idea what the answer might be and you can narrow it down to a couple of choices, guess; if you have no idea, just skip it. If you have a vague idea of what the professor is talking about, go ahead and try. Let him lead you to the answer! Once you start talking and pick up some momentum, you'll do better than you thought you would. If you have *no* clue what's going on, then save yourself the embarrassment and just pass.

It's okay to pass if you don't know the answer to a question a professor asks you. It's probably better for everybody. You save yourself the hassle of having to figure out what to say, and more importantly, you save yourself the risk of sounding like an idiot. Better yet, you don't waste the class' time or give them misinformation.

But if you're going to pass, do it *right.* Most students, when forced to pass their turn, put their heads down in shame and, with their lips quivering, give a lame excuse. "I'm sorry. I didn't read this case. I got confused and read the assignment for next week." They might as well say, "Please forgive me master. Show mercy on me." Come on; be a man. Or if you're a woman, be a woman. You don't have to ask for forgiveness or make up an excuse. You're an adult and you're paying a lot of money to be there. If you don't want to talk in class, you don't have to.

After all, what do you do when you go to the dentist and he tells you that you haven't been brushing or flossing properly? You don't feel ashamed, apologize, or make up an excuse. You just humor him a little and tell him you'll do a better job from now on. In reality, you couldn't care less what your dentist thinks about you. So why should it be any different with your law professors? You pay your dentist to clean your teeth, and you (indirectly) pay your law professors to teach you the law. If you have to pass, just be stern, look your professor in the eyes and tell him something like, "I'd rather not participate today." No shame, no excuses, no apologies; just an adult telling another adult to leave him the hell alone.

Professors Who Follow a Pattern. The third kind of professor is the one who calls on students against their will, but follows an established pattern in doing so. Therefore, a student knows in advance when he will be called on. For example, my Property professor during my first year of law school went down the class roster and called on students in alphabetical order. On average, she would get through three to five students per class session. Therefore, if your last name started with the letter S, once she started calling on the Rs, you knew your turn would be up within the next couple of classes.

My Civil Procedure professor—who happened to be the toughest professor I've ever had—divided the class up into several groups of about seven students each. Every day, one group would be responsible for answering all his questions. This way, you knew exactly when you would be called on, so you could study your ass off and be prepared. Nobody ever passed in his class, for two main reasons: 1) everyone was afraid of him; and 2) there was simply no excuse for not being prepared.

Though I would still rather take a class where only volunteers are called on, the classes where the Socratic Method works best are the ones where the students know in advance when they will be called on. This way, since the students are well prepared, discussion flows more swiftly, and class time is more efficient and productive.

The only detriment I can think of for this type of class is that students tend to get lazy when they know they won't be on call. For example, in my Property class, after I got my turn out of the way in the first weeks of class, it was pretty much a semester-long vacation. The way I see it, it's a pretty fair trade-off. Professors who call on random students keep everyone on their toes, so students are forced to always be somewhat prepared. But no student will be as prepared as he would've been had he known he would be called on. On the other hand, a professor who follows a pattern may have a lot of unprepared students sitting in his classroom, but at least he can be certain that everyone he calls on will be ready to answer just about anything he may ask.

WHAT COURSES WILL YOU TAKE

There are three types of courses you'll take in law school: required courses, non-required Bar courses, and electives.

Required Courses. For your first year of law school, you'll have no say in what courses you take. Some law schools might leave a slot open in a first-year student's schedule to pick an elective course, but the majority of law schools give 1Ls no liberty of choice. Not only can you not choose what courses to take, you can't even choose when—what day or time—to take them, or with whom. You'll be handed a class schedule, and if you don't like it, too bad. As I mentioned, some law schools differ slightly, but you can probably count on taking the following required courses during your first year: Civil Procedure, Contracts, Criminal Law, Torts, and Property, as well as a legal research and writing course. Constitutional Law is often a second-year required course.

No matter who you are, you have to take these classes. Each law school varies a little bit on what courses are required, and some may even have different names for similar courses. For example, a friend of mine went to a law school where Corporations was a required course. At my school, that course was called Business Organizations and it was a non-required bar course. At my school, Evidence was required, but at his school, it was an optional course in a (very important) bar exam subject.

Also, law schools can have different legal writing requirements. At my law school, students had to take a year-long legal writing course in their first year and an appellate writing course in the first semester of their second year. Other schools may impose additional or fewer requirements. For your sake, I hope your school requires as few legal writing units as allowed by the ABA. Legal writing classes in law school are a pain in the ass and demand an excruciating amount of busy work—with a tedious research or writing assignment due just about every week. It all leads up to a giant final project, such as writing a brief for a fictitious case.

No matter how stupid the writing classes may seem to you, don't blow them off. These courses usually consist of only one or two units, so the grade won't affect your GPA or class rank as much as other classes. However, when judges hire law clerks, or law firms hire summer associates, they often ask to see your legal writing grades, or they may even ask to see a copy of the final brief you prepared for class. After all, if you get one of these jobs during the summer, you'll spend countless hours doing research and writing briefs. Nobody wants to hire someone if they'll have to spend all summer teaching him how to write. Getting a good grade on your legal writing course lets employers know that at least one professor thought you were a good writer. This way, they don't have to take your word for it.

For your second year, you'll have fewer required courses, and you'll be free to choose electives. At my law school, 2Ls were required to take Evidence and Constitutional Law, as well as an appellate writing course. By this point, you'll have the liberty to make up your own schedule. So if you like to sleep late, you can take afternoon and evening classes. Or if a certain professor has a reputation of being an asshole, you can avoid his class. Most required courses are taught by more than one professor, so you can (usually) choose for yourself.

During your third year, you'll probably be required to take a legal ethics course. Other than that, you'll have likely taken all your required courses and should have plenty of room for electives.

Recommended Bar Courses. Bar courses are the ones based on subjects taught in the infamous bar exam. All of the aforementioned required courses, except for the writing classes, are bar courses. Apart from the required ones, there are several bar courses that are optional, although your school will encourage you to take them. Some law schools will require bar courses that are only electives in other schools. Also, law schools in certain states will offer certain bar courses that will be pretty useless in other States, since that subject might not be taught in that state's bar exam. For example, while law schools in California encourage their students to take a Community Property course, I doubt that schools in states that follow the common law for distribution of property (e.g., Massachusetts) would offer a Community Property course, much less require or encourage it.

At my law school, the following Bar courses were encouraged, but not required: Business Organizations (or Corporations), Wills

& Trusts, Remedies, Criminal Procedure, Personal Income Tax, and Community Property. While most of my classmates took all or most of these courses, I decided to take only Business Organizations and Wills & Trusts, because they were the only ones that seemed interesting to me. I have no problem taking a dull class if it's required. After all, if something is required, it's required; there's no getting around it. But I'll be damned if I'm going to voluntarily enroll in a course about a subject I care nothing about. There were plenty of other available elective courses that seemed much more interesting and useful to me.

There are two reasons why most law students end up taking all or most of the non-required bar courses. The first reason is because the law schools recommend that students take them. Law students tend to be docile, and unquestioningly do whatever their law schools say. If a law school were to order its students to shave their heads and commit mass suicide, I wouldn't be surprised if half the student body complied. The other half would only shave their heads, but decide in the end the suicide idea to be a bit much.

The second and more obvious reason is because students want to be as prepared as possible for the bar exam. This makes sense. The bar exam is extremely difficult and you need all the help you can get in order to pass. However, you shouldn't treat law school as a three-year preparatory bar exam course.

There are certain people who decide at a very early age that they want to become attorneys. When they go to college, they pick their major according to what they think will help them get into law school and excel once they're there. They tell everyone they want to be Pre-Law majors. What they don't realize is that universities don't actually offer Baccalaureate programs in Pre-Law, and even if they did, law schools say they prefer their prospective students not to enroll in such programs. They encourage prospective students to major in whatever field interests them most. At this point, these future law students become confused. They look up relevant statistics and see that the most popular former major in law school is Political Science. Political Science is a great field of study if you're interested in politics, but unless you practice in Washington DC, an attorney has little use for an academic background in politics. Still, if you visit a college campus and talk to all the political science majors, I'm sure you'll find that many of them are just putting in the requisite four years before they can get to law school.

My point—and my opinion—is that even if their goal is to go to law school, college students should try to get the most out of college and worry about law school when the time comes. A college student majoring in political science just because he thinks it will get him into law school is making a mistake. Had he majored in something that actually interested him, he could've still gotten into law school and would've enjoyed a more fulfilling educational experience.

The same goes for law students. Instead of focusing on law school and trying to get the most out of it, they're always thinking about the next step. From day one, they worry about where they're going to work after they graduate and how much money they're going to make. But before they can work and make money, they have to pass the bar exam. So they worry incessantly about the bar exam. Law school lasts three years; the bar exam lasts a few days. It's not like the Olympics, where people train for four years in order to compete in a race that's over in thirty seconds. The bar exam is hard, but you only have to start worrying about it and studying for it a couple of months in advance.

Anyhow, when you take a bar course in law school, it will give you a foundation for that subject, but it won't be nearly enough to pass the bar exam. You'll still have to study your ass off later. Besides, I don't know how good your memory is at retaining information, but after I took an exam for a particular class, I pretty much forgot everything within the next few weeks. For the bar exam, you'll probably have to go back and learn everything all over again. If you didn't take a certain bar course, the difference will be that you'll have to learn that subject for the first time, as opposed to learning it for the second time. You'll probably have to do a little more work than someone who already took that course, but it's definitely manageable.

Weigh the pros and cons and decide for yourself. The obvious pro is that you get an edge for the bar exam. Another pro to consider is that since the bar courses are so popular you will have no trouble finding commercial outlines for the specific subject and probably case summaries for your case book as well. This makes studying for these classes easier. Also, the availability of supplements, as well as the fact that the bar courses usually have so many students in them, make it plausible to skip class when necessary without any major repercussions.

On the other hand, the cons are plentiful as well. Bar courses tend to be more demanding than non-bar electives. The work load is usually heavier and the exams are more difficult. Plus, grades for bar courses are usually curved, so your chances of getting a good grade are significantly lower.

In the end, since the pros and cons seem to balance each other out, my suggestion is to take a course if the subject interests you, and you think you'll get something valuable out of the class. Forget about the bar exam for now and look at a course on its own merit. The law that governs business entities was an interesting subject to me and a field in which I wanted to learn, so I decided to take Business Organizations. On the other hand, I felt that Criminal Procedure had a strong chance of being as boring and useless to me as its required sister, Civil Procedure. I allowed myself the luxury of not taking it and never regretted my decision.

Electives. My favorite classes in law school were the non-bar electives, mostly because the structure and environment of these courses resembled the undergraduate classes I used to love. The class size is smaller, ranging from as few as ten students to as many as fifty students, depending on the popularity of the subject. The atmosphere in class is usually more relaxed and informal, and students are not as stressed out about being called on since there aren't as many spectators.

Also, elective courses often offer a superlative educational experience: the professors are almost always genuine experts in the field. This is also true of many of the bar courses, but sometimes, since bar courses need to be widely offered, available professors will be somewhat randomly assigned to teach them, regardless of their experience or training. For example, for my first semester of Constitutional Law, I had a young, newly hired professor whose expertise in the field was based on having taken Constitutional Law as a law student about ten years earlier. For my second semester of Constitutional Law, I decided to switch to another professors' class. Her expertise was based on the fact that she had taught the course

for about ten years. While this was more acceptable, ten years earlier she had been at the same level as my first semester professor. On
the other hand, the professors who teach the small elective courses
pretty much live for the subjects they teach. They have usually practiced extensively in the field, and many of them actually work as
attorneys within that specialization, teaching a class or two on the
side.

The best part about elective courses is that they give you the
freedom to study subjects that you actually *care* about. While some
law schools offer certificates of expertise in certain areas of law, the
majority of law students simply pursue a general law degree. When
I used to tell people I was in law school, they would often ask me,
"So what kind of law are you studying?" Or worse, "What's your
major?" When I told them that I was just getting a law degree, they
would look at me skeptically as if I was keeping information from
them, or like I was one of those unmotivated college students who
never declare a particular major and end up getting a general
studies degree. The truth is that law students don't specialize in
anything. In fact, most attorneys arrive at their specializations by
chance. After graduation, most law graduates take a job with
whoever hires them and do whatever work their bosses tell them to
do. Whatever field that work happens to fall under will most likely
become their area of expertise.

However, this doesn't mean that you can't be passionate about
a field of law and nurture your interest in it. That's where elective
courses come in. If you're interested in a particular area of the law,
you should look at the courses a law school offers before you
commit to it. If one law school offers more courses within that field
than the others, you might consider going there.

In my case, the area of law that interested me the most was
international law. Fortunately for me, my law school placed a strong
emphasis on this field and offered several relevant elective courses,
and I ended up taking: International Law, International Disputes,
International Business Transactions, and International Criminal
Law. I still couldn't tell people I was an International Law major,
but at least I was able to nurture my interest in the subject.

Finally, elective courses give you the chance to explore fields of
law that you might know little about, but you think might interest

you. Who knows, you might enjoy a certain elective and decide to venture into that field. At the very least, you will broaden your knowledge of the law and receive a better-rounded education. Some of the other interesting electives I took in law school were Family Law, Labor Law, Federal Indian Law, Intellectual Property, and Real Estate Finance.

Likewise, you should determine which courses are best for you, and choose those. And think about courses that truly don't interest you, and avoid those—without looking back.

6

Exams

One of the most important aspects of law school to understand and never, ever forget is that for every class you take, the only thing that really matters is *the exam.* It doesn't matter if you had perfect attendance, took great notes, participated in class, and answered all your professor's questions impeccably; if you fail the exam, you fail the class.

On the other hand, if you never went to class, didn't take notes, or passed your turn every time the professor called on you...*it does not matter.* If you get an A on the exam, you get an A for the class.

I never had a class like this in college. In undergraduate classes, grading was usually comprised of a few papers and a couple of exams or quizzes, as well as some consideration for things like attendance and participation. A professor would take all the scores and calculate a final grade. In law school, some professors may allot a few extra points for participation, and some may have a midterm exam in addition to the final. But I never had a law class where the final exam was worth less than 90%, and for the majority of law classes the final exam is worth 100% of the grade. So if you ever start to worry about falling behind in a class or you start to get cocky because you think you're ahead, remind yourself that *the only thing that matters is the exam.*

Some love this system and some hate it. Personally, I thought the system suited me perfectly. I really wasn't the model student when it came to class—I frequently skipped, often showed up unprepared, and rarely volunteered to participate. I was usually just another student on the roster, contributing little to the class, and never really getting much out of class time. However, when it came time to exams, I got my act together. Once classes ended and the reading period began, I underwent a complete transformation. I would lock myself in a room and study all day, every day until exams were over. By the time I entered the exam room, I guarantee you I was just as prepared as any of the students who read every case throughout the semester and lived to kiss the professor's ass, always raising their hands and going to office hours.

That's the beauty of this system. No matter what went on during the semester, everyone is now on a level playing field. If you kissed the professor's posterior all semester, it doesn't matter; you could have gotten in a fight with him to the same result. (Well, almost.) To avoid favoritism, exams are graded anonymously. So when a professor grades an exam, he doesn't know if it belongs to the girl who sat in the front row and was always quick to raise her hand, or if it belongs to the girl who sat in the back row and shopped for shoes online all semester.

But just as there are students who benefit from this system, there are plenty of students who fall victim to it. Since it all comes down to the exam, if you have a bad day, a whole semester can and will go down the toilet. All it takes is a couple of mistakes, and you could fail an exam, and maybe even flunk out of law school. That's exactly what happened to one of my classmates.

He never came across as an outstanding student, but it certainly surprised everyone when news broke out that he had flunked out of law school. During the semester, he appeared to study hard and he often participated during class. When finals came around, he didn't perform well, getting mostly Cs. And then came what I thought to be the toughest exam of my first year, written by the toughest professor I had in law school: Civil Procedure.

There was a typographical error in one of the exam questions which concerned the date in which an event occurred. Something was supposed to have occurred in the year 1998, but the professor mistakenly typed, "1988." My friend read way too deeply into the mistake and thought the question was mainly a statute of limitations problem. He proceeded to write an entire essay about a statute of limitations violation that didn't really exist. That essay comprised a third of the exam and he got zero points for it. The other two essays could've been written by a Supreme Court Justice and they still wouldn't have been good enough to make up for the zero. He got an F on the exam.

He tried to argue to the administration that he had failed the exam solely because of the professor's typo, so he should at least be allowed to take the exam again. It was no use. They didn't think the professor's mistake was "sufficiently material" to merit a second chance. After two semesters of working his ass off, he was told his grades weren't good enough to continue in law school.

All it takes is a little mistake, be it by the student or by the professor, and you're done. You might not flunk out of law school—you have to mess up pretty badly to get an F on an exam—but it's very plausible to go into an exam confidently and come out with a C- or a D. Even one of these will *really* hurt your grade point average and cause your class rank to plummet.

Always remember that *the exam is the only thing that matters for a class*. Everything else is just bullshit. Sorry to be crude, but this point is so important it needs to be emphasized. When you read a case decision, the only thing that really matters is the ruling on the issue at hand. Any other unrelated views that the judge expresses are called *dicta*. While *dicta* can have persuasive value, only the ruling is binding as legal precedent. In law school, the exam is the law. Everything leading up to it is just *dicta*.

THE EXAM FORMAT

There are two formats that law professors use for their exams: multiple-choice and essay. The majority of my exams in law school were solely essay. Several exams were a mixture of multiple-choice and essay; few were strictly multiple-choice.

Multiple-Choice Exams. Multiple-choice exams are self-explanatory. Unless you were home-schooled all your life and attended some sort of experimental college, you've probably taken more multiple-choice exams during your academic career than you can count. I liked multiple-choice exams in law school because they seemed easier than essay exams. When I say easier, I mean it in an entirely physical sense—you show up with a pencil and fill in bubbles, as opposed to being required to type enough words to write a novel. I finished multiple-choice exams quickly, and never felt exhausted when I finished, as I always did after an essay exam.

However, while I found multiple-choice exams to be less physically taxing, I got better grades on essay exams, or the exams that were blends of the two formats. With essay exams you have more control over a question, enabling you to take the answer where you want it to go. Even if you don't know something, you can steer your answer in a direction where you can input the information you *do* know. On the other hand, in multiple-choice, you either know something or you don't. You can always guess, but I'd rather take my chances breezing my way through an essay question rather than taking an all-or-nothing guess.

Also, multiple-choice exams allow professors to ask questions about anything and everything. Essay exams usually consist of only a few questions, so you usually only have to worry about the major concepts of a subject. The little details will probably be left out. But multiple-choice exams consist of dozens of questions, allowing the professor to cover much more ground.

For example, my Wills & Trusts exam consisted of 100 multiple-choice questions. This is a broad subject with a million little intricacies, so with 100 questions, just about everything was fair game. At around the 75th question, the professor, running out of things to ask, had no choice but to revert to the obscure far corners of estate law. I remember being stumped by a question on whether the State of Mississippi allowed the biological parents of an adopted child to inherit property from him if he died without a will. Had it been an essay question, I could've probably mustered up a decent answer. Since it was multiple-choice, all I could do was guess: "C."

You should also keep in mind that most law school exams are curved, so you know that professors have to make their multiple-choice exams *difficult*. Otherwise, if 20 people get every question right, the professor will be forced to give out 20 As. This would make the higher-ups angry and they would probably give the professor a stern lecture about making his exams more difficult.

Professors are given certain rules they have to follow when writing their exams. I'm sure professors would love to give short, easy exams. After all, they have to grade those things. I doubt any professor actually enjoys reading 100 different answers to the same question. Especially since those answers come in the form of 3,000-word essays written in an extreme hurry. There are certain length and difficulty requirements by which professors have to abide.

For my Constitutional Law class, I had a newly hired professor teaching in his first semester of law school. Leading up to the exam, he repeatedly told us that the test would consist of twenty multiple-choice questions. "That's *it?*" The whole class was delighted. Constitutional Law is a required bar-course and one of the harder and more important courses in law school, so everyone expected the exam to be pretty tough. Twenty multiple-choice questions didn't seem bad at all. The day of the exam, as I opened my exam packet, I read the following line in the instructions: *The exam consists of 20 multiple-choice questions and 4 essays.* Almost in unison, the whole class looked up at the proctor and said: "What the hell is *this?*"

Apparently our rookie professor had submitted an exam that the administration deemed too easy. They told him he had to either submit at least thirty more multiple-choice questions, or add a few essays. Personally, I've never written an exam, but I can assume it's easier to write four essay questions than 30 multiple-choice ones. For multiple-choice you not only have to come up with the question and answer, you need at least one or two realistic-sounding decoy answers as well. Our professor, pressed for time, threw in four essay questions but didn't bother to tell any of his students about the changes. A couple of students who went to his last minute office-hours found out about the change in the exam and managed to tell a few friends. But plenty of us were completely oblivious to the additions.

I showed up to the exam not expecting to be doing any typing, so I didn't even bring my laptop—just some number two pencils. I had to borrow a pen from a classmate and handwrite four long essays. My hand kept cramping up, and I was constantly distracted by the desire to find my professor and punch him in the face. When the exam was over, I knew I had bombed. I was right; I got a disappointing C.

Essays. Though you've taken essay exams before, essay questions in law school have a unique formula. They consist of hypothetical cases that occur in fictitious states, such as the State of Bliss or the State of Utopia, and feature characters with helpful names, like Peter Plaintiff or Debbie Defendant. While the names of the characters and states are unoriginal, some professors get really creative. I remember in my Torts exam, my professor came up with a tremendously elaborate hypothetical situation that included jet-skis, Boogie boards, sharks, drunken teenagers, a negligent lifeguard, and a whole bunch of serious injuries. I kept forgetting I was taking an exam, and felt like I was reading the weirdest news story of all time.

After all the facts are listed, there's a question and instructions on what to write. Usually, you'll be asked to do some role-playing. You might have to pretend that you're a clerk for the law firm that represents Peter Plaintiff. Using the facts listed, you'll have to write a legal brief explaining how good a case he has against Debbie Defendant. You then write an essay explaining how all the little facts apply to the relevant law. The most important thing is to spot all the legal issues that present themselves. Then you have to analyze each issue and weigh all the relevant factors. Professors give a certain number of points for each issue. If you analyze an issue to the fullest extent possible, you get the maximum points available for it. If you don't even spot the issue, you get zero of the available points. Then, after a professor reads the essay, he tallies up all the points for each of the issues.

Usually, an essay exam will consist of three or four essays. Or perhaps it will have one or two big essays, divided into a few subsections. Each essay will be worth a certain number of points. Professors are usually kind enough to tell you how much each essay is worth, so you know which ones to spend the most time on. After all the points are tallied up from all the essays, it's just a matter of comparing them with the rest of the class. Since most exams are curved, it doesn't matter how well you did, it only matters how much better or worse you did than your classmates.

Exam Technique Courses. Since the legal essay format is new to most first-year law students, private companies offer courses on exam-taking techniques. Such courses are offered early during first semester, usually take up an entire weekend, and are more than likely overpriced.

During my first semester, I was so busy during the week, that I really cherished my weekends. When I saw that an optional exam-technique course would take place on Saturday and Sunday from 8:00 a.m. to 4:00 p.m., I immediately decided that I would rather go to the beach and relax during my precious time off. I would figure out my own exam techniques. As you may recall, during my first year, I lived in an apartment complex full of 1Ls. When I woke up that Saturday morning, the place looked like a ghost town. It seemed as if there had been a nuclear holocaust and I was the only survivor. I walked up and down the grounds of the complex, and tumbleweeds rolled in front of me. For a few minutes, I thought I might've been dreaming, but then I remembered that the exam-taking technique course was that weekend.

Apparently, I was the only student in the apartment complex— and one of the few of the entire first-year class—that opted to pass on the course. Naturally, I worried that I might've missed out on crucial information, and that it would leave me a step behind the competition. I quickly forgot about this once I arrived at the beach and had a splendid time relaxing on the sand, enjoying the sun, and swimming in the ocean. You would've had to handcuff me and drag me in order to get me into some stuffy, windowless classroom to attend an eight-hour seminar.

That night, I asked some of my classmates if they wanted to go out to the bars with me. "No," they responded responsibly, "I have to get up early for that stupid exam seminar tomorrow." I went out without them and had a great time, and on Sunday, I went back to the beach. By the end of the weekend, I was refreshed and ready to tackle another week of law school. My classmates were all burnt out from the course, and needed another weekend to unwind from their weekend. On Monday, they all had bags under their eyes, while I had sunburn on my nose.

Still, a part of me wondered and worried whether I should've gone to the seminar. I asked one of my friends who had attended the course what he had thought of it. He told me, "Actually, it was pretty worthless. All they did was emphasize IRAC the whole time." IRAC is a handy formula that stands for Issue, Rule, Analysis, and Conclusion. This means that when writing an essay for an exam, you should: spot the ISSUE; state the RULE of law; take the relevant facts and form a legal ANALYSIS; and after you've weighed all the factors, state your CONCLUSION. It's pretty simple, and it hardly merits a two-day seminar.

His girlfriend, who had also attended the course added: "We also had to take mock exams. That was pretty helpful." I can see how that would be helpful, and give you a feel for the exam format.

However, just about every professor in law school posts copies of his old exams, either online or at the law library. So if you ever want to take mock exams, you have plenty of options. Many professors will even be willing to look at your answers and tell you what they think. This way, you not only get a feel for the general format of law school exams, you actually get a feel for your specific professor's format, which is much more important.

Some people like to get all the help available and be as prepared as possible. If that's the case, go ahead and take the course. Also, if you're just going to spend all weekend watching TV or masturbating, then you might as well take the course. It would probably be a better use of your time. But if you're like me, and you can't really get through a week unless you have those two days to relax and enjoy yourself, then let me assure you: you don't really need the course. It might be helpful, but you can figure out everything your classmates learned on your own. If you do a little extra work, I doubt they'll have any real advantage over you come exam time.

There's just one exception I should mention: LEEWS. If you're considering a seminar to take, this might be the one, since it takes just one day and seems reasonably priced (and I've heard that it is worthwhile). Better yet, if you're not up for the local seminar you can buy the LEEWS CDs. (No, I don't get paid for this "plug.") In retrospect, since I probably would've skipped it anyway, maybe I should have bought the CDs and listened to them at the beach. I could have gotten the benefits of attending the seminar *and* kept a suntan.

STUDYING FOR EXAMS

Personally, I think a seminar on how to study for exams would be much more useful than one on how to take them. How well you study for an exam will determine how well you do. The hell with IRAC—if you don't know what you're talking about, you might as well use IRAQ with a Q, or IRAN with an N, or even SAUDI ARABIA. Unfortunately, as far as I know, nobody offers a course on how to study for exams. Oh well, I probably would've skipped it anyway.

Coming into law school, you will hear classmates talk about two study tools: case briefs and class outlines. During your orientation, before classes start, you might even have to attend a class that teaches you how to do each. At my orientation, we had a class to teach us how to brief a case.

Case Briefs. Essentially, a case brief is a synopsis of a case decision. After you read a case, so as not to have to read it again later when you forget all about it, it helps to jot down a few sentences that capture the main gist of it. This is—or should be—an obvious and simple concept. But, at my orientation course on case briefing, the instructor made it seem as if knowing and using the proper formula for briefing a case was integral to one's success in law school. Terrified, all the students began paying close attention and taking notes. We were instructed that a proper case brief should always include the following categories:

Procedural Posture: How and why the case arrived to the respective court. A detailed listing of who sued whom, how the lower courts ruled, who appealed and how.

Facts of the Case: A listing of the events that occurred leading up to the law suit.

Issue(s): What issues were brought to be decided by the court.

Law Applied: What body of law (statute, rule, prior case decision, etc.) was used to determine the case.

Analysis: How the court applied the law to the case's facts and issue(s).

Ruling: What the court ruled.

"Wow," I thought, "that's a pretty extensive formula." All of a sudden a few sentences to capture the main gist of a case had turned into a whole bunch of busy work. When I did the reading for my first class, it took me a long time to read the cases, but it took me even longer to brief them using the tedious formula I had learned.

Nevertheless, I persevered, and for every one of the several cases I read, I made a nice, long brief with all the requisite categories filled out.

When I got to class and the professor started talking about the first case, I pulled up the brief on my laptop. The professor mentioned a few important things from the case, asked a few questions about some of the issues, and moved on to the next case. "Wait! Hold *on*," I wanted to shout, "What about the procedural posture? What about the body of law that was applied? You mean I did all that work *for nothing?*"

I certainly did. None of that crap matters, and including it in your briefs is not only a waste of time, it will also defeat the purpose of your briefs—to capture the essence of a case so you don't have to read a bunch of text later.

You will never be asked to turn in your case briefs. Nobody will ever see them except for you. Their only purpose is to help you study. Therefore, you don't need someone telling you the proper formula on how to brief a case, because there *is* no formula. After you finish reading a case, write down what is important in a few sentences. Write down only what you will need to know from that case in a few months when you go back to it as you're reviewing for exams.

The exception to this is if you know you'll be on call for a particular case. Then, you might want to write a more detailed brief, so you'll be able to answer a broader range of questions. Otherwise, the main gist from a case is all you'll need to know.

Individual cases aren't really that important for exams. All you need to know is the law. Professors just use cases as a tool. What you're really supposed to be learning is the law that stems from the cases. I guarantee you that come exam time, the detailed facts of a particular case will not matter in the least bit. If you ever come across a question on an exam about the procedural posture of a case you had to read, type the following answer in bold letters: *You are an [fill in your favorite expletive here]!* Don't get too excited. You'll never get a chance to write that answer because a professor will never ask a question about procedural posture, or about any other mundane detail.

For an exam, all you need to know is the law, so your case briefs should include just that: what the court ruled and the law that was established. You might also want throw in a few of the case facts to put everything into context. Anything beyond that is useless busy work.

For an assignment during my third year, I had to give a presentation with a small group of classmates. As we were preparing, we started talking about a particular case, so a girl in the group pulled up a brief on her laptop. I peeked over to her computer screen and couldn't believe what I saw: she was still using the exact formula she had learned at orientation, three years before. She had every category filled in, even procedural posture. I can only assume that she used that formula to brief every case she ever read. I can't imagine the countless hours she spent going back to a case after reading it to find the information for her precious categories. All that useless busy work...*oh,* the horror.

You don't have to follow my advice; it's just my opinion. Maybe you want more information in your briefs. If that's your style and you feel like it's the best system for you, I encourage you to do it. But please feel free to steer away from a formula that an instructor gave you during orientation. First-year law students are confused and don't know what to expect, so it makes sense for them to absorb any advice given to them by an authority figure. But as you trudge through law school, you'll start to figure out what works best for you. Forget about what people have told you. Hell, forget about what I've told you. Find what system works best for you.

Class Outlines. A class outline takes everything covered in a course, shaves off all the unnecessary details, and narrows itself down to the crucial things you need to know. A good class outline is a fundamental tool for success in an exam. The problem is that people's opinions differ widely as to what constitutes a good outline.

They say one of the hardest things for an artist to know is when to stop painting. How does an artist know when to step back and be satisfied with his work without adding another brushstroke? If he stops painting too soon, the canvas will seem incomplete; if he paints too much, it will seem as if there's too much going on. The same goes for outlines. They have to be the right length and contain the right amount of information. A law student has to learn when to stop adding to it.

Some people have outlines that are way too long, defeating their own purpose. If you're going to compile *everything* into an outline, then it's not really an outline. You might as well just study off your textbook. During my first year of law school, one of my neighbors had a 70-page outline for one of his classes. I guess he bragged about it to someone, and word began to travel. When people heard about it, they felt intimidated and inadequate about their own outlines. Everyone thought, "Should my outline be longer? Am I missing some information?"

I was sitting with a few of my friends, when someone came up to us and told us the gossip. Seeming a bit nervous and excited, he told us: "Oh my God. Did you guys hear? That guy's outline is seventy pages long!" We were pretty surprised by the high number of pages, but none of us knew how to respond. Was a 70-page outline better than a 20-page one? Was a long outline good, or just redundant? Finally, one of my friends spoke up, "So? My Gilbert's outline is *200* pages long." We all laughed, but my friend had a good point. An outline is supposed to save you the hassle of flipping through a bunch of pages. It's not supposed to contain all the information available. Otherwise, you could just save yourself the extra work and buy a commercial outline like Gilbert's or Emmanuel.

The only situation in which a 70-page outline might be useful is in an open-book exam. Some professors allow students to bring their books, notes, and outlines to an exam. But no professor will ever let you bring a commercial outline. Therefore, if an exam is open book, it could be useful to have a detailed outline, containing anything you might ever need to know. That way, nothing will stump you. Then again, if your outline is too long, you'll spend half your allotted exam time flipping through pages. If your outline is *really* long, you should invest the extra time and make a labeling system with tabs dividing up the different sections. This way you'll be able to find what you're looking for quickly, and you won't waste any precious time during the exam.

While my neighbor with the 70-page outline represents one extreme, the other extreme is well represented by a law student I met from a school in Washington, D.C. He told me that his method was to have the shortest outline possible. He would start with a fairly long general outline and keep trimming it down until he was left with a final outline that fit onto one page. His final outline wouldn't actually contain any information. It just contained short descriptions of all the main concepts. All the actual information would be stored in his brain. He used the outline simply to refresh his memory and point him in the right direction. In other words, his final outline probably looked like a copy of the class syllabus that the professor hands out at the beginning of the semester.

From hearing the two contrasting stories, who would you guess did better in his exams, my neighbor with the 70-page outline, or the guy with the one-page outline? Go ahead and guess without reading ahead. Actually, it's a trick question. They both did extremely well. My neighbor got excellent grades for his first year and transferred to one of the top-ranked law schools in the country. I didn't keep in touch with him after that, but I assume he continued to do well. When I talked to the guy from D.C., with the single-page outlines, he had just graduated at the top of his class and was about to start working with a top firm in Los Angeles.

I guess the moral of the story is to figure out what kind of outline works best for you. Personally, I think a median between one and 70 pages is the best bet. A good outline should lie somewhere between the class syllabus and the textbook. It should be well-organized and contain all the main concepts. Within the main concepts, you should include whatever information you think is important. This is when you have to learn to stop painting. Don't add every piece of information available, because in that case, you could just make a Xerox copy of your Gilbert's outline. Once you get a good grasp on the material, you can go ahead and trim your outline. Or it might be a good idea to keep two outlines, one with a ton of detailed information, and a more concise one that just guides you through the main concepts.

Getting an Outline. But what do you do if you're just too damn lazy to make an outline? Don't worry, there's hope for you too. Luckily, while you may be too lazy to make an outline, chances are that most of your classmates are not. Therefore, it's only a matter of getting someone else's outline. Unfortunately, law students are as protective of their outlines as a lioness is protective of her cubs. They are never willing to just give them away.

There are two main reasons why law students hold on to their outlines so tightly. The first reason is because they work very hard on them, and they don't just want to hand them over to someone who'll enjoy all the fruits of their labor for free. You may be thinking, "That's fine; I respect the 13th Amendment. Someone should be compensated for their work. How much do I owe you for the outline?" Unfortunately, due to the second reason, it's not that simple. The second reason law students are protective of their outlines is that, since exams are graded on a curve, nobody wants to help out their competition. It's like giving a weapon to your enemy before going to battle against him. Therefore, getting a good outline from someone usually takes a little bit of tact, and a lot of charm.

If you're an attractive girl, then you should have no problem. Just go up to the ugliest, nerdiest guy in your class, flirt with him for a couple of minutes, and—just as his testicles are about to burst—ask him if you could take a look at his outline. Not always, but usually, the ugly, nerdy guys have *very* good outlines. If you think this sort of tactic is beneath you and you have too much integrity to do such a thing, brace yourself, you're going to have a hard time as an attorney. If you're a good-looking guy, I guess you could try the same approach. Unfortunately though, while the ugly, nerdy *girls* in law school tend to have very good outlines as well, they aren't nearly as desperate as the ugly, nerdy *guys*. It will probably take more than a few minutes of flirting.

But what if *you're* ugly? What if you're one of the nerdy guys with whom hot girls mistakenly flirt in order to get an outline, when—little do they know—you're just as desperate for one as they are? In that case, you have to have something to offer. Nobody will take pity on you and give you an outline just because you're ugly. Well, almost no one. However, if you have something that a law student wants, you'll find they will be much more willing to help you out.

It's like in *The Godfather.* When Vito Corleone does someone a favor, instead of accepting payment he requests that they be willing to return the favor in the future. In law school, people will only do you favors if they think you might be able to repay them in the future. If your father is a senior partner at a prestigious law firm, everyone who knows will be nice to you, since one day they might need you to put in a good word for them. Exchanging an outline for being in the good graces of a big-shot senior partner's progeny seems like a reasonable trade.

If you're ugly and your father is a bum, well, you'll have to figure something out on your own. One of my friends in law school was a huge pothead and he cleverly used it to his advantage. He was generous with his weed, always willing to share it with anyone who wanted to smoke with him. It was no surprise that by the end of a semester, his generosity paid off. He usually had to sort through a dozen outlines to see which one he liked best.

Personally, I never liked asking others for their outlines, but if someone offered one to me, I would accept it graciously. I was fortunate enough to have some good friends who never really bought into the whole competition thing. If I ever had a class with them or took a class they had previously taken, they would email me their outlines—no questions asked.

There was one occasion in which I asked someone for an outline, and I learned never to do it again. During my first-year orientation, the incoming students were split up into small groups, and each group was assigned to a second-year student who was supposed to be some sort of mentor. My group was assigned to a girl who wasn't shy about telling everyone that she was at the top of her class. She took a particular interest in me and told me that if I ever needed anything to be sure to ask her. (She meant *anything*.) When she learned we had the same Contracts professor, she told me, "Oh, I should give you my outline for that class. I got an A on the exam."

Being just a rookie, I was still unfamiliar with the politics of law school. I appreciated the gesture, but I didn't realize its magnitude. The outline of the student who set the curve in a class the year before was *extremely* coveted. She knew this; I didn't. She emailed me the outline and asked me not to share it with anyone. I thanked her, but I still didn't see the big deal about the outline. I finally realized how valuable it was when it came time to study for the first semester exam. The outline was extremely helpful, and though I didn't get an A, I would've done much worse without it.

The problem was that Contracts was a two-semester course, and she had advertently only sent me the outline for first semester. By the time second semester exams rolled around, I had pretty much lost touch with her. I didn't see her often, and when I did, it was just a matter of crossing paths between classes and saying "Hello." Besides, I had gotten the impression that her interest in my success was not exactly pure. Her motives behind giving me her outline were apparently romantic. I had a serious girlfriend whom I married the following year, so I wasn't available. This made her angry.

Still, Contracts was a difficult class, and I needed a good outline. So I decided to ask her for the second semester outline. I wrote her a nice, polite email saying how much I had appreciated her first semester outline and how helpful it had been. I made up some bullshit about how I was lost in the class and I was having trouble putting my own outline together. I also made sure to remind her that she had been assigned to be my mentor and I needed her help. I sent the email out with a prayer; I desperately needed this outline.

She replied promptly with a very brief email. In fact, it contained exactly two words. It read: "No. Sorry." I was so pissed off I could've killed her. Worse, the whole semester I had kind of expected to get the outline, so I had slacked off more than usual. Now, I had a *lot* of work to do toward my own outline, and little time to do it.

I ended up getting a C. Naturally, I blamed my mentor for my bad grade. If she had given me her outline, I would've done better. Of course, I probably would've also done better if I hadn't expected to get an outline from someone else, and made my own. But it's always easier to blame others rather than yourself.

At least I learned a valuable lesson about the politics of law school. She was Vito Corleone, and she had done me a favor. (Come think of it, she was overweight and Italian, so she did kind of *look* like Vito Corleone.) When I didn't humor her romantic feelings for me, I failed to return the favor. The next time I needed her help, it was no longer available. A good outline is like muscle for a gangster. If someone gives you their outline, unless they're your good friend, then they're using that muscle to get something in return from you. It's probably best that you make your own outline. You won't fall into debt, you'll actually learn more by doing it yourself, and who knows, it might pay to have a little muscle of your own.

PERFORMANCE-ENHANCING DRUGS

Professional athletes live under a constant pressure to perform at their peak physical condition, and their livelihood depends on how well they perform. Therefore, it's no surprise that many athletes turn to banned substances for performance enhancement. In 2003, the BALCO scandal devastated Major League Baseball's image. No Olympics—summer or winter—would be complete without a few doping scandals. And I remember being distraught when my childhood idol, Diego Maradona—the Argentinean equivalent to Michael Jordan—was ejected from the 1994 World Cup after testing positive for a banned substance.

Other than carrying heavy textbooks, law students aren't required to perform strenuous physical activities. Maybe there are a handful of law students out there who are really into a recreational sport, and feel the need to take steroids or other supplements; but that's a small minority. One thing that is certain is that law students are forced to undergo rigorous mental activities: reading, thinking, studying, and exam taking. Law students use their brains as much—if not more—than baseball players use their muscles. Therefore, if baseball players feel the need to use steroids, it seems natural that law students would feel the need to take a substance that would enhance their mental abilities.

While pharmaceutical companies have yet to market a wonder-drug that makes you smarter, they market plenty of wonder-drugs that help you concentrate better and stay awake longer. In other words, everything a law student could ask for when he's studying for exams. Though it's not really talked about very much, there is a wide use of prescription drugs to enhance performance within law schools, especially during exams. Drugs like *Ritalin* and *Adderall*—routinely prescribed to hyperactive children—have become to law students what EPO is to professional cyclists.

I'm not going to stand on a soapbox and moralize. If a student feels the need to boost his abilities chemically, that's his prerogative. After all, plenty of law students drink alcohol and use recreational drugs, so they might as well take drugs that help them study. I've never heard any sort of official announcement or talk by an administration about law students doping. Perhaps if such drug use becomes more prevalent, law schools might start to address it. They might even make alterations to the no-cheating honor code. It would be hilarious if it got to the point where random urine tests were performed after exams, like in the Olympics. Those who test positive would fail the class.

Many of my friends used *Ritalin, Adderall,* or similar prescription drugs, and they claimed that the effects were beneficial. They said it allowed them to study more efficiently and for a longer period of time. They even took pills during exams—especially the long essay ones—to help get through them.

Of course, as is the case with every medication, there are side effects. One of my friends, who happened to get good grades, used *Ritalin* regularly, especially around the time of exams. One day, he approached me with a worried look and told me, "Man, I haven't been sleeping very well lately. I don't know if it's because I'm nervous about exams, or *what*. I've only been sleeping like two hours a night. And then in the afternoon I feel exhausted."

I didn't have to think about it very long. "It's probably the *Ritalin,*" I told him. He looked at me like a little kid having just heard that Santa Claus didn't exist, and it was his *parents* who put presents under the tree. A sad truth, painful to hear, but it made a whole lot of sense. He had been so excited about his precious *Ritalin* that it never occurred to him that it could be bad for him. He was studying well, understanding everything, and getting amazing grades. Don't get me wrong, he was a smart guy, and I'm sure he would've done well without the *Ritalin,* but it certainly made things easier for him.

Personally, I stayed away from pills. To keep me awake while studying for exams, I relied solely on coffee and *yerba mate*—an ultra-caffeinated, but natural, herbal tea from South America. I tried *Ritalin* once when my friends offered it to me, but I had a bad experience with it and ended up hating it. Four of us were studying for an exam at a friend's apartment, when everybody popped a *Ritalin* pill. I decided to join them. You can call it peer pressure if you want to get after-school-special about it. I just didn't want my normal, human brain to get left behind by their three chemically altered, super-brains. So I took the pill and washed it down with about five cups of coffee.

By the time the *Ritalin* and the caffeine took effect, I was absolutely wired. I felt like I could've translated the entire U.S. Constitution into Latin while doing push-ups. (And I don't even speak Latin.) I felt like a computer ready to intake whatever information came my way. Hell, I could've taken the exam right then and there. I could've figured everything out on the spot and written an infinite number of essays.

I was ready to study, but my friends, who were more accustomed to the effects of *Ritalin,* had a different idea. "Let's break for lunch," one of them suggested. "Yeah. Good idea," the others agreed. Before I could disagree, we were all on the way out the door and into my friend's car.

"Wait a minute," I thought. "I've never felt more like studying in my entire life. I can't waste this moment. Forget lunch; I have to *study!*"

"Hey guys," I announced, "I'm actually going to stay and study." They said okay, and left without me. I returned to my friend's apartment, but when I went to turn the doorknob, it was locked. I ran back to the parking lot, but my friends had driven off. I searched my pockets but realized I had left my car keys and cell phone inside the apartment. Worse yet, I had left all my books, laptop, and study materials inside the apartment as well.

I was stuck outside my friend's apartment with nothing to do and nothing to study. All I could do was sit and wait for my friends to return. I don't know if you have any experience with amphetamines, but when you're tweaked out of your mind, the last thing you want to do is sit there and wait for someone to arrive. My friends took their sweet time with lunch. They took about an hour and a half to get back, but to me it seemed like an eternity. By the time they returned, the effects of the *Ritalin* and caffeine had worn off and I was feeling burnt out and angry. On top of that, I hadn't gotten any lunch so I was hungry too. I really didn't feel like studying anymore. I decided that day that *Ritalin* was not for me, and I never took it again.

STRESS

Exams make law students *very* nervous. So much is at stake that the pressure tends to make people crazy. In my opinion, feeling a little pressure is a good thing. It forces you to study harder and approach the exam more seriously. However, too much stress is a bad thing and it will likely hinder your performance.

I believe it was Benjamin Franklin who said that the two things in life that were certain were death and taxes. He should've added a third: the fact that around the time of exams, law students are absolute stress cases. A combination of nerves, lack of sleep, and being burnt out from studying too much leaves everyone looking like a zombie. They sweat profusely, their faces become pale, massive bags form under their eyes, and they tend to act all jittery and nervous—much like Woody Allen acts in all of his movies. They talk fast and seem as if they're always in a hurry to get somewhere or get something done. They're a mess.

The Law Library. The best thing you can do to avoid this kind of stress is stay away from other law students. If you like to study with a small group of people, that's fine. But when you study alone, find somewhere where you can actually be alone. Or at least somewhere where you can be away from other law students. In other words, stay the hell away from the law library.

The only times I went to the law library during exams were when I had to print out my notes and outlines, since I didn't have a printer at home. While I was there, I would stick around and study for a while, but it was impossible for me to concentrate. It resembled a bad zombie movie where Woody Allen had been hired as the acting coach. It would be difficult to find a worse environment in which to study.

It was always the same thing. As soon as I would sit down, the zombies—smelling fresh flesh—would pick their faces up from their books to see who it was. Someone would recognize me and make his way over to my desk. Inevitably, a nervous conversation would ensue about exams, how much they sucked, and how we couldn't wait for them to be over. These conversations were strange and awkward.

During my first year, in the days leading up to my Civil Procedure exam, I was at the law library when one of my classmates approached me. I had talked to him before, but he was hardly a friend of mine, or barely even an acquaintance. He came up to me looking as if he was about to cry.

"Hey man," he greeted me, but didn't even wait for a response, "...do you understand this *Erie Doctrine* shit? I've been working on it for three days straight and I still don't get it. I mean, just when I think I'm starting to get it, I read something else about it and I realize that I don't really get it at all."

He wasn't asking me any questions, he just needed someone to vent to, like a two-minute therapy session. As he spoke, he stared off blankly into space behind me, with a sad, almost suicidal look about him. I don't think he even knew who he was talking to. I thought he was having some sort of panic attack and I got the impression he was about to faint. After a few awkward seconds of silence, I had to say something. "Yeah," I nodded my head, "It's pretty hard."

That was it. He turned around and left. Probably went off to find another classmate to vent to. For the rest of the time I was there, I couldn't stop thinking about the weird encounter. I even doubted whether *I* understood the *Erie Doctrine* as well as I thought I did. If that guy was so freaked out about it, then maybe there was more to it.

Avoid the law library. You don't need to feed off of others' stress too. You'll probably be stressed out enough on your own. Find a place where the only stress that can distract you is your own.

The Exam Room. While you can avoid other law students when you're studying, unfortunately, you won't be able to avoid them when you take exams. This is the point when law students reach the peak of their stress levels. The nervousness of your classmates might distract you during the minutes leading up to the exam, but don't worry, once the exam starts, you'll forget about any external stimuli. You'll become so focused on what you're doing that a terrorist could blow himself up on the other side of the room and you wouldn't notice. You would ignore the pain from the shrapnel and the dying screams of the wounded around you, and keep typing away.

The day of the exam, you should try to get to the exam room at least half an hour early. As an undergrad, it had never even occurred to me to get to class early on the day of an exam. Therefore, when my first law school exam was scheduled for 9:00 a.m., I showed up at 8:45 a.m. and thought, "I hope I'm not too early." On the contrary, I was the last one there. The classroom was packed and everyone had their game faces on, and their laptops up and running. The only seat left was the one directly under the air conditioning duct, which every other student had carefully avoided. I froze my ass off during the exam. At one point, my hands became so numb, that I had to assume my fingers were hitting the keys as I typed.

You should especially be there early for an exam if you plan on using your laptop. If it's a multiple choice exam, or you're a masochist and you choose to handwrite an essay exam, you can probably show up a few minutes before it starts. But if you're planning on using a laptop, you should get there early to set everything up.

I have never been to an exam when somebody's computer didn't malfunction. There are always one or two poor souls who have problems with their laptops. The proctor will start reading the exam instructions and someone will raise their hand with a look of panic on their face. *"Uhm,* my computer's not working," they'll announce with what little composure they have left. Most law schools have a few computer geeks on hand to help the poor souls. However, the proctor will not wait for any computer problems. If the exam starts and your laptop isn't running, you'll have to grab a blue book and a pen, and start writing.

Worse yet is when someone's computer breaks down during the middle of an exam. You have to grab a blue book and pick up where you stopped typing. You can only hope and pray that the computer managed to save whatever work you had completed up to that point. Otherwise, your professor will only grade what you were able to turn in.

As the luck of the draw would have it, I had my own turn at a computer mishap. Fortunately, the problem occurred before the exam started. Unfortunately, it happened right before a really long essay exam. My law school used a pretty archaic computer program for exams that required you to save everything to a floppy disk. Since the people who designed my laptop figured nobody used floppy disks anymore, they didn't bother to install a floppy drive on it. I was forced to buy an external floppy drive for the sole purpose of using it for exams. Being a poor law student, I bought the cheapest one I found. I used it for about a year and a half, exclusively for exams. Then one day, the floppy drive just decided to stop working.

I got to my exam early and set my computer up. The program was unusually slow to load, until it courteously told me—with about five minutes remaining before the start of the exam—that my floppy drive was unable to read the disk. I desperately motioned for one of the computer geeks to come over and help me. He pressed a few keys, pressed a few more keys, and finally pointed to my external floppy drive. In his infinite geek wisdom he said, "That thing's cheap."

With that diagnosis, he couldn't do anything about it. Before I could feel sorry for myself, or yell at the computer geek, I heard the proctor say: "You may begin the exam."

I pushed the computer geek out of the way, and ran to the proctor's desk to pick up a blue book and a pen. If I ever develop carpel tunnel in my right hand when I'm older, I'll be able to point to the exact moment when it was triggered. I had to handwrite one of the longest essay exams I took in all of law school. My hand kept cramping up, my pen was running out of ink, and by the end, my handwriting was so illegible that I could barely read my own scribbling. I could envision my professor grading my exam, throwing his arms up in the air and saying, "This idiot needs to get a laptop."

The result of my computer malfunction was a *very* disappointing C. I'm sure that if my stupid floppy drive had worked my grade would've been at least a letter grade better.

It might not seem so, but it's easy to get thrown by any disruption to your routine. Whether that is indeed the cause of a bad grade, it will *feel* that way. So it pays to get to the exam room early to ensure that you can be fully prepared once the exam begins. You can make sure that your computer is working properly, pick a good seat, and even review your outline a few final times. But there is one major downside to being early for an exam: you have to put up with your nervous classmates. Before an exam, I like to get into a zone and be absolutely focused on what I'm about to do. This becomes challenging when you're sharing a room with fifty people making nervous small talk.

If you thought the law library was bad, an exam room during the minutes leading up to the exam is about twenty times worse. It resembles a scene in one of those epic war movies, like Braveheart, right before the troops go into battle, and before Mel Gibson manages to inspire hundreds of soldiers without the use of a microphone. Everyone knows what's coming, but they don't know what fate they'll meet. Everyone is anxious and afraid for their lives.

Since nobody knows what to expect, the first exam of the first year is by far the one that inspires the highest levels of anxiety. My first exam was Criminal Law, and as you may recall, I decided to show up fifteen minutes before it started. Being an entirely new experience for me, after I sat down, I had no idea what to do next. Since the girl sitting beside me had been there at least a few minutes longer and looked as if she had everything under control, I assumed she would be able to help. "Hey," I asked her, noticing she already had a copy of the exam, "Are they handing those out, or do we have to pick them up?"

"They're handing them out," she answered curtly, without even looking at me.

I noticed some instructions written on the chalkboard that said something about inserting a floppy disk into your computer before turning it on. "Hey," I asked again, "What about the disk? Where do we get it?" This time, increasingly annoyed, she turned toward me and explained, "There's a lady going around, handing everything out."

About two minutes went by and I still hadn't gotten my exam or my floppy disk. Again, I leaned over to ask one final question: "Hey. Are you sure that lady's handing the stuff out? I don't see her anywhere."

Having had enough, she exploded. "I don't know! Ask the proctor. You should've gotten here earlier. You need to calm down and leave me alone!"

The type of person I am, if I have any sort of confrontation with someone, I spend the next few hours thinking of things I should've said. So during the exam, my mind would occasionally wander from the specifics of criminal law to what I should've said to that bitch sitting next to me. My thoughts quickly traveled from, "Intoxication is only a defense if it eliminates the *mens rea* of a crime," to, "I should've just told her to fuck off. How can *she* tell *me* to calm down, when *she's* the one yelling?"

It was *highly* counterproductive. I kept having to shake my head and remind myself that the exam was worth 100% of my grade. There would be plenty of time to wish death upon neighbors later.

Though I was slow to forgive that girl for our pre-exam confrontation, I can understand why she yelled at me. She was probably trying to concentrate and keep all that information fresh in her head, and my questions were distracting, or at least annoying. I imagine she felt bad or maybe embarrassed for yelling at me like she did. It probably even caused her mind to wander during the exam, just as mine had. Still, when I got my grade back for that exam—a big, fat A—one of my first instincts was to find that girl and rub it in her face. In the name of good sportsmanship I decided against it, though I made sure she found out through alternative channels.

For another one of my exams, the tables turned and I found myself in that girl's position. I had gotten to the exam room early and picked what I thought would be a good seat. I always liked to sit on an aisle seat, so there couldn't be more than one person sitting next to me. Then, I would spread my stuff out far to the other side, so hopefully, nobody would sit in the chair directly next to mine. I'm not anti-social; I just don't like people to be near me during an exam.

I thought I was safe in my carefully planned seat, until about twenty minutes before the exam started. A friend of mine arrived, saw me, and came over to sit next to me. This guy was an overweight sports fanatic who happened to have gone to college at my alma mater's top athletic rival. Therefore, every time we talked—instead of, "Hi, how are you?"—he would start our conversations with, "You think you'll beat us in basketball this year? At least we kicked your ass in football." I was trying to keep my mind on all the information I had crammed into my brain the last few days, but as soon as I saw him, I knew he would cause my focus to shift toward the subject of collegiate sports. As soon as he sat down, he started, "How's the recruiting going for next year? I heard you guys were getting a seven-footer."

I like sports, and I try to keep up with what's going on. Under normal circumstances, I would've at least humored him and feigned interest. But never have I cared less about college basketball than at that moment. Indiana University could've somehow gotten Michael Jordan to come out of retirement and Wilt Chamberlain to rise from the dead, and—in violation of all of medical science and NCAA regulations—signed them to play on the team. Then and there, I wouldn't have cared. Still, unlike the girl in my Criminal Law exam, I remained poised despite my annoyance. "I have no idea," I told him. He proceeded to lecture and enlighten me about college basketball and football for the next fifteen minutes. When the proctor announced, "You may begin your exam," I thought, "Finally! Now he'll shut up."

So what should you do if you want to get to the exam room early but you don't want to be distracted by your classmates? I suggest that you get there early, find a good seat, and set everything up. Then, once you're ready, get the hell out of there. Find a quiet spot outside the building and hang out there until a few minutes before exam time. By the time you get back to your seat, you'll be focused and ready to begin.

WRITING PAPERS

As far as I know, there's only one way to avoid exams in law school. You can take classes that require you to write a paper in lieu of an exam. These are usually the smaller elective courses, since bar classes are required to have exams. Some people who dread exams love the idea of a paper class. As an English major in college, I must've written hundreds of papers. Most of my undergraduate classes required them instead of exams. Since I had so much experience writing papers, I thought I would be better off taking paper classes in law school. However, papers in law school are an entirely different animal.

First of all, they're long as hell. In college, most of my papers were between 10 and 20 pages long. I had little trouble writing them the night before they were due. In law school, most of my papers had a 50-page minimum. You have to be on some serious methamphetamines to write a 50-page paper in one night. For law school papers, I usually ended up spending about two weeks researching, and another two weeks writing. I never spent four weeks studying for an exam—not even for my hardest ones. Usually, one week of good efficient studying was enough. The beauty of an exam is that it comes and goes fairly quickly. You know when it will be held, and more importantly, you know when it will be over. Once it's over, even though you may want to go back and change some answers, you can't. It's out of your hands and you're better off never thinking about it again. But papers have a tendency to linger. Some professors may even require you to hand in a rough draft a few weeks before the final paper is to be submitted. This means that you'll work your ass off to get something down on paper, only to have your professor cross half of it off with a red pen, and tell you to write it again.

First, you do all the research. When you're sick of researching, you start writing. When you're sick of writing, you start revising and re-writing. When you're done with all the writing and re-writing, you have to go back and make sure you cited everything correctly. Law professors are *very* picky about the way you cite, and everything must follow the direction of the *Blue Book*—the Constitution of legal writing. Only then can you print the paper, have it bound, and turn it in. By the time the final paper is out of your hands, you've probably done enough work to cover three exams.

So if a paper requires so much work, why not just stick with exam classes? The big benefit of writing a paper is that it tends to give you much more control over your final grade. With an exam, you can study your ass off and know everything but still make some dumb mistakes and mess up. Just like that, even though you were well-prepared, you can get a bad grade. Your chances of success are drastically lowered by the fact that most exams are graded on a curve. On the other hand, with a paper, you'll rarely be surprised by the grade you get. If you're honest with yourself, you should know exactly how good your paper is and what grade it deserves. Most professors will be glad to look at drafts and tell you what needs to be changed. You can rewrite your paper until your professor tells you it is good enough for an A. And don't worry, I've never heard of a professor curving papers.

Do you remember my friend who failed his Civil Procedure exam and flunked out of law school? Well, you'll be happy to know that he persevered and bounced back. He was forced to sit out a semester and take the baby bar (California's First-Year Law Students' Examination). When he passed, he was allowed to resume his studies. Having developed a bit of an exam phobia after his bad experience, he resorted to taking as many paper courses as possible. He told me he tried to take at least three paper classes a semester. He admitted that it was a lot of work, but at least it gave him a sense of security and kept his GPA up.

Personally, starting with my second year, I tried to take one paper class per semester; no more, no less. I thought taking more than one would be too much work. There's nothing worse than writing two papers simultaneously. If you're not careful, you'll mix the two papers up and neither one will make any sense. By taking one paper class, I could be sure to get at least one good grade per semester and be able to deposit it toward my GPA.

Finally, if you decide to take a paper class, make sure it's in a subject that interests you. The last thing you want to do is write a 50-page paper on a topic you care nothing about. The paper will write itself *very* slowly and your lack of enthusiasm will seep through to the reader—the professor—who happens to have dedicated his life to that subject.

If, however, you choose a subject you are interested in, that mutual interest will usually carry you a far part of the way, and it won't seem nearly so bad as those three exams you could have taken with the same effort.

7

LIFE OUTSIDE LAW SCHOOL

After finishing a law school exam, an alcoholic drink will taste better than it ever has before. There's nothing better than a few drinks to help you unwind after so much mental strain. After an exam, I strongly encourage you to take the rest of that day off and drink with your friends. If you don't drink, then do whatever it is that helps you unwind. Anything, as long as it's not related to law school. Many people, after finishing an exam, take a couple of hours off and start studying for the next one. That's a mistake; after so much strain, your brain needs a night off.

Sometimes you don't really have a choice. You might get unlucky and have exams on consecutive days. In that case, you'll just have to suffer through it. Law schools are usually pretty good about scheduling exams, however, so students won't commonly have them on back-to-back days—or worse, two in one day. If you do have a scheduling conflict, some schools may even allow you to reschedule an exam for a more reasonable time slot.

In your first year, you definitely won't have any exams on consecutive days. You'll probably have at least one or two days between exams. In that case, I suggest that after you finish an exam, you have a few drinks, unwind, and forget about the exam you just took. The next morning you'll feel refreshed and ready to study for the next one.

DRINKING AND PARTYING

After my first semester Torts exam as a 1L, some friends and I decided to drive to the coast, where my friend's parents had an enviable beach house. We still had one exam left before the winter break, but we thought a little ocean air and a lot of alcohol would recharge us for the last exam.

My torts exam was a bitch. It was three-and-a-half hours long, and when the time elapsed, I still had a lot of writing left to do. I miscalculated my time and ended up spending *way* too long on the first essay. By the time I got to the third and final essay, I had to rush through it, leaving several issues unmentioned.

When I left the exam room I was exhausted and angry. My professor, who was actually a very nice guy, was waiting outside to ask his students what they had thought of the exam. Naturally, since law students tend to be obnoxious ass-kissers, everyone had kind words to say to him. Lying to his face, they told him what he wanted to hear: "It was challenging but reasonable. I actually enjoyed it." When he asked me what I had thought, I looked him in the eyes blankly and told him, "It was *way* too long. Three and a half hours and I still didn't finish." He got a sad look on his face, as if I had just told him his daughter was ugly. I walked away just as an ass-kisser tried to make him feel better, "It wasn't *that* long. I thought it was the perfect length."

I was upset about my performance in the exam and I kept thinking about it all the way to the beach house. My friends kept trying to console me, mostly because they were sick of hearing me whine about it. It wasn't until I finished my fifth beer and moved on to the sixth that I started to forget about Torts. My mood improved, I started laughing, and I stopped bringing everybody down. I kept drinking.

After losing count of how many beers I had, we moved the party to the hot-tub. We soaked in it for about an hour, until the alcohol, hot water, and all those bubbles began to team up against me. I had never given much thought to those warning signs on Jacuzzis that try to dissuade users from drinking while soaking. Apparently, there's a reason for those warnings. I started to feel sick and realized that I was about to vomit.

Without giving a warning or announcing my intentions, I jumped out of the hot-tub and ran toward the house, hoping to make it to the bathroom. My friends, puzzled by my abrupt and seemingly arbitrary exit, probably thought that after being in the hot-tub for over an hour, I had suddenly realized how hot the water was. I ran across the yard and onto the patio with some time to spare, confident in my chances of reaching the toilet. But I encountered a problem: there were about ten sliding glass doors, and only one of them was unlocked. In my drunken stupor, I had forgotten precisely which of the doors was unlocked.

I could feel the vomit coming up, so I frantically tried to open each of the glass doors. From left to right, I tugged on each door as hard as I could, but none of them would budge. My confused friends watched me from the hot tub, wondering what the hell I was doing. When I finally couldn't hold it any longer—after pulling on about seven uncooperative doors—I gave up on the idea of reaching the bathroom, turned around, and threw up all over the patio. The type of mess I made could have significantly brought down the house's property value.

Happy to finally have an explanation for my strange actions, my friends all began to laugh. After I finished vomiting and my friends stopped laughing, one of them yelled out to me from the hot-tub, "Are you alright?"

"Yeah," I responded with vomitus dripping from my chin, "I finally got all the Torts out of my system."

Alcohol. Studies repeatedly show that of all the professions in this country, lawyers tend to be among the leaders in problematic alcohol consumption. (Dentists often compete for the top spot. I guess something about staring into the mouths of strangers all day makes you want to pour vodka down your own). It makes sense that many lawyers become alcoholics when you consider how stressful the legal profession can be, and how mind-numbingly boring an attorney's job can become. But I doubt attorneys start drinking in response to the stress and boredom of their careers. This probably just intensifies the drinking. I'm willing to bet that any lawyer with a drinking problem was well on his way toward alcoholism during his three year stay at law school.

Alcohol is a big part of extracurricular life in law school. While there's probably more alcohol consumed by undergraduate students in universities, drinking seems to be more acceptable in law school. In college, since most students are under the legal drinking age, administrations usually try to regulate drinking to some extent. While they can't stop their students from drinking themselves blind on their own time, they can at least prohibit the consumption of alcohol on campus by minor students. In law school, with the exception of the rare Doogie Howser-like genius, almost every student is over 21. Therefore, the administration has no real issue with students drinking alcohol. Hell, getting drunk is part of what being an attorney is all about.

During my orientation, before first-year classes started, a big meet-and-greet party was organized on campus. All first-year students, as well as professors and members of the administration, were invited to attend and drink free beer out of several kegs. There's nothing quite like alcohol to encourage a bunch of strangers to meet and greet each other.

I remember sitting there, talking and drinking with a few of my new classmates, when the Dean walked by, nursing a pint of beer. "Hi guys," he introduced himself, as if we didn't all know who he was, "I'll be your dean for the next three years." We all stood up straight and started acting and speaking very unnaturally, like you do when you meet your girlfriend's parents for the first time. "Guys, this is my daughter," he introduced us to his attractive, college-aged daughter who, unlike her father, was *not* holding a glass of beer.

Normally, we would've remained stiff and reserved until the Dean left, but a combination of the alcohol and the sighting of an attractive girl transformed us from a group of polite law students into a bunch of cheesy guys at a bar. The Dean went from being the most important person in the room to the equivalent of a barstool. We all turned our backs to him and started talking to his daughter. The questions flew: "So, do you think you'll go to law school here?" "What's the Dean like at home?" "Can I get you a drink?" "Does the Dean approve of you dating his students?"

Regret was visible in the Dean's face, though I'm not sure what he regretted most: coming to the party, bringing his daughter, or green-lighting the decision to serve alcohol. At the very least, I assume he regretted introducing his daughter to a bunch of near-drunk guys—even if we were his law students. He chugged the rest of his beer, excused himself, and dragged his daughter away with him. That was the only time I ever talked to him directly, until he handed me my diploma at graduation.

Social Functions. There are two main kinds of functions held at law school: ones held during lunch-time and ones held in the evening. The lunch-time functions are usually short meetings, lectures, or seminars. They almost always offer a free lunch or snacks to those who attend. This maximizes attendance, since about half the people present are there mainly to be fed. The amount of money law schools spend on delivery pizza for such events must closely rival the amount they spend on salaries.

The functions held in the evening are more social in nature. They are often fundraisers consisting of dinner and dancing, and of course, drinking. Alcohol is served, and the advertisements for the event are always sure to mention that drinks will be plentiful. Otherwise, no one would go. My law school had two major evening functions every year, a silent auction in the fall and a formal ball in the spring. They were the equivalent of the homecoming dance and the prom in high school. People would talk about these events in anticipation for weeks: "Are you taking a date?" "Are you going stag?" "What are you wearing?" "Where are you going to drink before?" "Where are you going to drink afterward?"

On the night of these events, people would drink as if it was the last night before prohibition. Once the alcohol was depleted, everyone would head to a bar and keep drinking. By the time the bars closed, crazy things had happened, and come Monday, people would be inevitably afraid to show their faces in class. Drunken fights would erupt, drunken romances would spark, and drunken things would be said that couldn't be taken back after sobering up.

During the silent auction in the fall semester of my first year, one of the big prizes up for auction was a lunch date with Johnny Cochrane, O.J. Simpson's star defense attorney in his circus-like murder trial. After performing a minor miracle in getting his client acquitted when the whole world was convinced that he was guilty, Cochrane became the most celebrated trial attorney in the country. Having lunch with Johnny Cochrane for a law student was like a basketball fan getting to shoot hoops with Michael Jordan.

By the time the big prize came up for auction, we had all been drinking heavily for a few hours. A couple of my friends, thanks to the alcohol and the fact that they felt rich and powerful in their nice suits, threw any economic caution to the wind, and began to bid recklessly. Since the lunch date was open to three law students, three of my friends pooled their resources and became determined to share a meal with Johnny Cochrane at any cost. A 3L standing across the room was equally drunk and determined. As the bidding war climbed higher and higher, the auctioneer became excited. *"Sixteen-hundred!"* he shouted, "Do I hear sixteen-fifty?" When the bidding reached $2,000, he grew so excited that he became slightly deaf.

"Two thousand *fifty!"* my friend yelled, but the auctioneer didn't hear him, *"Sold* for $2,000 to the gentleman in the gray suit."

My friends were outraged. "We bid two-*fifty,"* they yelled as they charged up to the stage. A shouting match ensued between my friends and the declared winner and his friends. People got in each other's faces and grabbed one another by the collars. Had Johnny Cochrane's mother been alive, she would've been extremely proud to see a bunch of well-educated white men fighting for the right to have lunch with her son.

The issue took several weeks to resolve. Who was the real winner of the auction? If witnesses had heard my friends bid, but the auctioneer hadn't, did they lose the auction? It seemed a complicated matter. However, the morning after the auction, once both parties had sobered up, they realized how ridiculous the notion of paying $2,000 to have lunch with Johnny Cochrane was. Two-thousand dollars might be spare change to Johnny Cochrane, but it's a lot of money for a law student.

As the matter was being resolved by the auction organizers, my friends and the other guy each tried desperately to get out of paying for the lunch date. In a once-in-a-lifetime rarity, law students were actually trying to argue that they had *lost,* and the other party had won. Finally, the other guy—who after three years of law school was a more experienced litigator—put up a better argument, and convinced the organizers that he had lost the auction. He argued that since the goal of the auction was to raise money for a good cause, the prize should go to my friends, since they had bid $50 more.

So my friends had an hour-long lunch date with the one-and-only Johnny Cochrane, and were stuck with the $2,050.00 tab. It was a costly, drunken mistake. After the lunch, I asked my friends what it had been like. One of them said, "It was pretty cool. He talked about hanging out with Puff Daddy in St. Tropez."

Sadly, a few months later, the great Johnny Cochrane passed away. My friends were sad since someone they had met had died. But a part of them was satisfied. The fact that no one would be again able to have lunch with Johnny Cochrane made their prize seem more valuable. Their drunken mistake now seemed like a reasonable expenditure.

Parties. Aside from the evening functions organized by law schools, there are plenty of less formal gatherings at which law students drink excessively. Every Thursday, my law school's Student Bar Association held a "Bar Review." There actually wasn't much organization to it, they just announced the name and address of a bar, and everyone who felt like going *out* would show up. These Bar Reviews were a lot of fun early in the year, when many people attended. But as the semester went on and exams neared, people began to lose interest. At that point, instead of an event, it seemed more like you had run into some people you knew at a bar.

There are also occasional parties, get-togethers, and outings. It's not like college, where just about every night you can choose between a house party or the bar with the best drink specials. But if you like to go out, you shouldn't have a problem finding a few fellow law students to join you.

Surprisingly, one of the craziest parties I've ever been to was at law school. It was my first year and, along with a few of my friends, we went to a party thrown by a 3L at her house. Although she had cleared all the furniture out of her living room in order to create a make-shift dancehall, people were much more interested in gathering in the backyard. The guests were particularly intrigued by the swimming pool and a large grapefruit tree in full bloom beside it.

As the alcohol took effect, a large water and grapefruit fight ensued. People were pushing fully-clothed partygoers into the swimming pool. Once they were in the pool, others would throw grapefruits at them. And I don't mean soft underhand lobs; these were hard, baseball-style pitches with full windups. Nobody was safe. Anyone who congregated outside was fair game to be thrown into the pool and/or be pegged in the face with a grapefruit. Of all the fruits in the world, I can only think of a few which I would less rather be hit with—maybe a coconut or a pineapple would be more painful.

After the last of the grapefruits had been plucked from the tree and thrown at someone, the party began to die down. As my friends and I were about to leave, we stumbled upon an unconscious guy lying on the floor in the middle of a hallway. We thought he might've been knocked out by a grapefruit, but he had just had too much to drink. We poked at him, and asked him if he was alright, but there was no waking him up. We alerted the owner of the house, and she suggested that we move him to a couch so he could be more comfortable. Trying to be good Samaritans, two of my friends and I picked him up by the arms and legs, but as we lifted him off the ground, the guy regained consciousness. Remembering the evening's prior events, the guy, with good reason, thought we were messing with him. He probably thought that if he didn't take quick action, he would end up in the bottom of the swimming pool. So he started squirming and kicking like a fish out of water, causing us to drop him on the floor.

I try to imagine what must've been going through his head— waking up in a random house, being dragged away by three strangers—and I think I probably would've reacted in a similar way. He freaked out, and came after us like he was fighting for his life, cursing at us, and throwing wild, drunken punches in all directions. My friends and I evaded him, and he was too drunk to chase after us. Since he couldn't punch *us,* he decided to punch an easier, more stationary target: the wall beside him. He wound back and threw a vicious punch at the wall as hard as he could, putting his fist and half his arm right through it.

The owner of the house, who watched the whole thing, was horrified. First, her grapefruit tree gets stripped, and now some drunk guy punches a hole through her wall. This was not what she envisioned when she decided to invite a few law students over. Anyone who ever tells you that law students don't know how to party was not present that night.

INTERACTION WITH NON-LAW STUDENTS

As long as it is kept under control, going out and drinking can be good for you. It's a great way to release all the stress and relieve the strain a law student deals with throughout the week. You can have a great time with your law student friends, but after a while, inevitably, all conversations will end up being about law school. On a Friday night, after a week of going to class and reading cases, the last thing I wanted to talk about was law school. Still, if there was at least one other law student present, no matter how hard we tried to avoid it, the topic of conversation would steer toward law school. We would end up talking about our classes, professors, or classmates. All I wanted was to forget for the moment that I was a law student, but it was impossible.

While law students can be fun to hang out with, I recommend that you keep a few civilian friends on reserve. Law school can be overwhelming and all-encompassing. If you're not careful, it will take over your life. That's why it's important to socialize with people from the outside world, who don't know anything about the law school world, and don't care.

It can be hard to make non-law student friends, especially if you go far away from home for law school. This was true for me since I moved from Indiana to California. Fortunately, one of my good friends lived a few hours drive away from me. This guy was as far from a law student as you could get. His only experience with the law had been a drunk-driving arrest a few years before I met him. About once a month, when I was fed up with being a law student, I could drive a few hours, visit him, and escape for a weekend.

He owned a sailboat, so we would sail all day, and go out bar-hopping all night. The most we would talk about law school would be a short, requisite conversation where he would ask me, "How's law school?" I would say, "It sucks." And he would respond, "Yeah, well, you'll make a ton of money one day." That was it. No details, just a brief mention. After that, we would talk about all the other infinite things that go on in the outside world that law students don't make time for. By the time Monday came around, I had to be reminded when and where my classes met. It was exactly what I needed to refresh my brain and keep me going for another month.

Dating. It is especially important to interact with non-law students when it comes to dating. If you date a fellow law student, there will be no escape from law school's death grip. Not even during sex—the one time in life when no man or woman should think about the law—will you be safe. At the point of orgasm, you might unwillingly yell out an obscure legal term in Latin like, *"malum prohibitum."* The only thing more embarrassing than that would be if your mate, in turn, responded with, *"malum in se."* Don't know about you, but I can't think of anything *less* sexy.

During my first year of law school, my girlfriend was finishing her undergraduate degree in Florida. Although we lived in opposite sides of the country, our daily phone conversations and frequent visits were extremely helpful to my sanity. If you let it get under your skin, the first year of law school can be maddening. Being able to talk to someone on the outside every day was a priceless commodity, taking my mind off all the pressure and stress. Without the relief our conversations offered, I might've dropped out.

During my second year, after my girlfriend graduated, I realized that the only way to get her out to California was by marrying her. I spent most of the first semester of that year busy planning a wedding in Florida, and the second semester enjoying life as a newlywed. It was tough juggling law school and marriage, but again, it was nice to have a distraction. There was something going on in my life that was bigger than law school. I wasn't a law student who got married; I was a married guy who happened to go to law school.

During my third year, my wife and I had a baby. At this point, as you can probably imagine, law school occupied a small corner in the back of my mind. We rented a little duplex by the beach, and had a great time watching our little daughter grow up. I worked out my schedule so I would only have class twice a week, but I became so indifferent that even *that* seemed like too much.

On the other hand, two good friends and classmates of mine met, fell in love, and got married within their three years in law school. When people ask my wife and me where we met, we can smile, blush a little, and tell them we met in Paris—the city of light, the capital of love. For the rest of *their* lives, when asked the same question, my friends will have to shrug their shoulders and say they met in law school—the antithesis of romance, where love comes to die. Don't get me wrong, they had a great relationship and were very much in love. But although they never confessed to screaming out Latin legal phrases during sex, law school was a big part of their relationship. They took most of the same classes, so they could never get away from each other; worse yet, they could never get away from law school.

One time, I went over to their apartment to study for an exam with them. The place felt like a small replica of the law library, with the stressful air of exam season ever present. Whenever I finished studying, I could always talk to my wife about something else. Actually, I had no choice. If I talked to her about my exams, she would've either not known what I was talking about, or not cared. But after my friends finished studying, they had no one to talk to except themselves. Inevitably, they would talk about their exams, especially since they took all the same classes. Obviously, their upcoming exams would be the biggest thing in their minds, so talking about anything else would be like ignoring a pink elephant in the room.

Resisting love is futile. When Cupid's arrow strikes, it can't be ignored. So if you fall in love with a classmate, go ahead and pursue it. If anything, you'll be with someone who knows exactly what you go through every day. But if you have some control over it, I recommend that you look for love outside of law school…far, far away from it.

8

FINDING A JOB

I would guess that the majority of law students aren't there for sheer academic enjoyment, or intellectual stimulation. They are much more concerned about eventually getting a good job and earning a good salary. You can write about the pursuit of social justice and other well-minded topics in your admissions essay. But let's be honest, most people become lawyers because they want to be rich.

There was an older guy in my class who was probably in his late 50s. He was a bit of a charlatan, with a propensity to tell what seemed to be very tall tales. Still, if only half of the things he said were true, it appeared that he didn't really need to become an attorney to be successful. He claimed to have held a series of important corporate jobs, and acted as if he had earned and saved a good deal of money.

Since he was twice as old as most students in the class, and appeared to have been perfectly successful without the help of a law degree, there was no good reason for him to be in law school other than personal academic pleasure. I don't think he was too concerned about getting a good job after graduation. After all, starting a legal career when you're 60 doesn't seem too promising. What firm would want to hire a guy who's a few years from retirement, with no legal experience? He just seemed to really enjoy learning about the law. He was always willing to participate and was enthusiastic in class discussions. The novelty of having a older, loudmouth classmate wore away pretty quickly, however, and after the first few weeks everyone found him to be incredibly annoying.

I can assure you that my elderly classmate was a minority within law students. Not only because of his age, but because he was not consistently stressed out about finding a job. Even before the first day of class, law students are worried about what job they will get after graduation. After all, the reason most people are there to begin with is that they couldn't find a good, satisfying job after college. Therefore, almost everyone in law school has high hopes of landing an important job that will pay them a lot of money. Oftentimes, these high hopes end up driving law students crazy.

If you're thinking about going to law school because you want to land a high-paying job, let me warn you: nobody's giving jobs away like Halloween candy, where you just knock on someone's door, yell "Trick or Treat!", and they give it to you. It's more like Easter, where you have to hunt for it. Only in this case, the Easter Bunny is *really* protective of his candy, he hides it really well, and once you find it, you have to beg him to let you even taste it, much less take it home.

If you look at admissions brochures and websites, or if you visit a school before you commit to it, law schools make it sound as if included in the price of tuition is a guaranteed job after graduation. This couldn't be further from the truth. The only thing schools really do to help you find a job is open the doors to recruiters looking to fill positions. If you go to a top school, the doorways will be wider, and more recruiters will get in. I didn't go to Harvard or Yale, but it sounds as if for every job their graduates take, there were a few others for them to turn down.

I went to a mid-level school, and I can guarantee you that *very* few people, if any, were turning down jobs. At my school, the top 15% of the class tended to get interviews with recruiters, with a smaller percentage receiving subsequent job offers. Everybody else was left on their own to find a job.

This is where it really pays to go to a reputable school. If you rank at the top of your class, no matter what school you go to, recruiters will be interested. Considering it mathematically, if your school were to get one recruiter, then chances are he would be interested in the one student who is atop the class. If there were two recruiters, the top two students would be likely to get chosen, and so on. (It's never quite so tidy, but you get my point).

If you go to Harvard, there will be so many recruiters that even the guys with Cs might get a few interviews. The best firms will only consider the top students from the top schools, but there are plenty of firms that would love to display a few Harvard grads as associates—even if their grades suck. After all, a client may see your diploma hanging from the wall in your office, but I doubt he would ever see your transcript.

If you go to a less reputable school, you'll have less leeway. If you want recruiters to come after you, you're going to have to keep your grades up and rank high within your class. Otherwise, you'll have to bypass the in-school recruiting and find a job on your own. This means more work on your part, and probably less money. Obviously, if a firm is coming to you for a job, you can ask for more money than if you're going to them.

Summer Jobs

The whole job search starts with summer jobs. Do you remember as a kid when summer vacation was the greatest time of the year? For a couple of months you could run around and play all day without a care in the world. You would look forward to it all year, and when it finally came, you knew you could relax and enjoy yourself. Sadly, for law students summer vacation means just the opposite. They anticipate the coming of summer vacation—not with excitement, but with anxiety and yet more stress.

Law schools usually break for summer in May and fall classes usually start in late August or early September. Law students start to think about what they're going to do that summer no later than September. When it finally comes, relaxing is the last thing they want to do. For law students, the more work they do during summer, the better.

First Year

The summer after first year is not as important as the summer after the second year. Most firms hire summer associates during the summer between their second and third years. This too depends upon the school: the higher the law school in the rankings, the more likely recruiters will consider its first-year students.

Most law students thus try to use the summer between first and second year as a résumé booster, so they can land a good job the following summer.

Clerkships. Though not impossible, it is rare for most first-year law students to obtain a well-paying summer job. Most have to settle for unpaid internships or clerkships. Traditionally, the ideal summer job for the well-to-do 1L is serving as a clerk or judicial intern for a judge—the higher the court, the better. Before you get your hopes up, you should know that U.S. Supreme Court Justices don't hire first-year law students as their clerks. They hire from a pool of the brightest recent graduates from Ivy League law schools who are ready to kill each other for the positions. Federal Circuit Courts are probably out of the question too. But first-year applicants can serve as summer clerks in a variety of federal, state, county, or municipal courts.

If you ask me, clerking for a judge sounds like one of the worst jobs imaginable, especially since they don't even pay you. If it's a higher court, a clerk might receive a small stipend, but most first-year clerks do it for free. You'll do all of a judge's dirty work—all the tedious research and writing—while he plays golf, and later takes all the credit for your hard work.

A friend of mine, who annoyingly followed all the traditional steps of the well-to-do law student, served as a summer clerk for a judge in San Francisco after his first year. When I asked him how he liked his job, he told me he hated it. He said, "Do you remember our legal writing class? Do you remember the final assignment for that class? Well, it's pretty much like having a couple of those assignments due every day." Our grade for the class was based on a major brief we had to write for a hypothetical case scenario. The assignment was a gargantuan pain in the ass, and the thought of ever having to do another one like it—not to mention, a few a day for an entire summer—made me shiver.

Worse than the work was the fact that, not only was he not compensated, he had to somehow pay the absurdly high rents in San Francisco. He had to sell his soul to a student loan company in order to work his ass off for a judge all summer.

Of course, there are benefits to being a clerk. Law students don't just do it for the sake of tradition. My friend scored some terrific baseball tickets whenever the judge—a season-ticket holder for the San Francisco Giants—had more extravagant ways to spend his time. He also got to sail around the bay a few times on the judge's luxurious sailboat.

But what if you clerk for a judge in a land-locked area without a professional sports team? Basically, you earn the right to add some valuable experience to your résumé, as well as a weighty letter of recommendation. Whether that's worth spending an entire summer of your life stuck in a stuffy office, working your ass off for no pay, is entirely subjective. If you land a position as a clerk, brag about it. If you don't, be happy you didn't, and enjoy your summer.

Study-Abroad Programs. I didn't even apply for a clerkship. First of all, I'm opposed to the idea of working for no money. It's un-American, and the 13th Amendment explicitly prohibits it. Volunteering for a good cause is one thing, but America's judges aren't exactly starving African children—they could afford to pay their summer clerks a few bucks an hour.

Aside from that, I love to travel. If I go more than a couple of years without leaving the country, I get antsy. Therefore, I thought the perfect thing for me to do that summer was a study-abroad program. I would get to travel, have a good time, and get school credit for it. Law schools offer plenty of summer abroad programs all over the world. Some consist of simply taking classes in a foreign law school, while others feature some form of internship.

Many people assume that such programs will be expensive, but they're actually quite reasonable. In fact, taking units abroad usually costs just as much as taking units at your home campus. The only difference in price will come from airfare and possibly from living accommodations. But if you go to school somewhere where rent is expensive, like California or New York, there's a good chance you'll actually save money overseas.

These programs are open to all first- and second-year law students from accredited law schools. The only question is whether your law school will grant you credit for them. My law school offered several summer-abroad programs, and took great pride in them. So much so that they had a stingy policy to refuse credit to students who underwent summer-abroad programs through other schools. The problem was that, while my school had plenty of programs to choose from, I liked one from another school the best.

I found a program in Buenos Aires, Argentina. Since I still have family who live there, I try to go back and visit every few years. I was due for a visit, so I thought this would give me a perfect excuse to go. Additionally, I was low on money, and with so many eager relatives offering free food and shelter, Buenos Aires was the only international spot where I could spend the summer rent-free. Plus, thanks to a favorable exchange rate, the few dollars to my name would magically triple in spending power.

Since the program was through another school, I had to get special permission from the Dean of Students to receive transfer credit. She had a reputation for being a little cold-hearted when it came to granting favors to students. Some friends of mine had wanted to do a summer-abroad program in Hungary through a different school and she had refused them credit for it. As much as I wanted to go to Argentina, I had decided I wouldn't go through with the program if it wasn't for credit.

My friends, after their request for a credit transfer was rejected, said, "To hell with the Dean of Students and her precious credits." They went ahead and did the program in Hungary regardless. To me, that seemed like a waste of time and money—especially since they weren't really interested in the academic program, as much as in the idea of spending the summer in Eastern Europe. What's the point of participating in a scholastic program if you won't get credit for it? I guess you can put it in your résumé, but it's not like a clerkship; it won't impress most recruiters. In that case, unless it was a particularly fascinating program, forego it and travel with your own itinerary. You would save money and be free to do whatever you wanted.

During my appointment with the Dean of Students, I told her that since I spoke Spanish and had lived in South America, I was particularly interested in Latin American law. Currently, my school only offered programs in Europe and Asia. While those programs seemed perfectly interesting, they wouldn't gear my education in my desired path. It was a convincing argument; she bought it. She authorized me to receive full transfer credit for the summer program in Argentina.

I had a great time that summer. Classes lasted for a month, and I received four credits. I met dozens of law students from Argentina and all over the United States. After the program was over, I stayed there for another month—visiting family, eating steak, and enjoying the fine Buenos Aires nightlife—and I even found the time to backpack around Bolivia and Peru with my brother. Even though critics of my résumé may not agree, that summer between my first and second years of law school was one of the greatest of my life. How many law students can say *that?*

SECOND YEAR

The summer between your second and third year is the crucial one. This is when law students compete for the ever-coveted summer associate positions. This is when, for the first time, your hard work can start to pay off. Summer associates aren't "clerks," and they sure as hell aren't unpaid interns. Summer associates, in big firms, make a lot of money. Depending on the caliber of the firm, they can make between $5,000 and $15,000 a month for the three months of the summer that they work. It's roughly the equivalent salary at which you would start, should they hire you permanently after graduation.

As nice as it is, the money is not the real allure of summer associate positions. The experience is good, the bragging rights are better, and the salary is probably more money than you will have ever earned up to that point. But what law students cherish most about being a summer associate is that if you perform your tasks well, don't mess up too badly, and don't do anything stupid—like spill hot coffee all over a partner's suit—you'll probably be invited to come back after graduation as a full-time associate. Just like that, your law school (and maybe lifelong) goals can be clinched after two years and a summer.

Once you're offered that permanent job, you can take your foot off the gas pedal and coast. All you have left to do is graduate and pass the bar exam; then you're set. You can start fantasizing about what you'll do with all that money you'll be making. You'll need to get some nice suits. Maybe you can even start looking for a house to buy. *Oh,* one more thing: enjoy all this free time and daylight while it's still available to you, because you won't be seeing much of either after you start working.

But don't get ahead of yourself just yet. Landing a summer associate position is tough. Impressing your bosses and being asked to come back as a permanent associate, tougher still.

On-Campus Interviews. The hunt for summer associate jobs starts immediately at the beginning of the second year. Before the summer is barely over, you have to start worrying about what you'll do the next summer. Early in the fall semester, law schools hold on-campus interviews (commonly referred to as "OCI"), where recruiters come looking for potential employees. A list is compiled with all the firms that will be sending recruiters, and each firm explicitly states what requirements candidates must meet to be considered.

When I looked at this list, I was impressed by how long it was. I thought, "Wow, with this many firms, there should be enough jobs for everybody." But upon closer examination, I realized that most of the firms were only accepting applications from students in the top 10% of the class. I compiled my own list, setting aside the few firms with more lenient standards, who might take a chance on someone at the top 25% to 30% of the class—right about where I stood. This list was considerably shorter. I did the math. If the top 10% of the class had such a long list to choose from, and the other 90% had such a pathetically short one, my chances sucked.

Some of the firms have additional, annoying requirements. Many ask that candidates be involved in law review, or at least moot court. Law review is a journal published by law schools featuring boring essays about esoteric legal concepts. While law schools vary in their requirements to qualify for law review, students are usually selected on the basis of their first-year grades and their performance in a spring write-on competition—where students are given a legal issue and are required to write a paper concerning it. The students selected become members of the law review, earning the right to add that title to their résumés. Of course, this comes at the expense of doing a bunch of extra work throughout the rest of their law school years.

Personally, while I like to write, I don't care much for academic writing. I find it too forced, unnatural, and incredibly tedious. I especially hate academic legal writing. I made a conscious decision in my life that the less legal writing I did, the better. Hence, I passed on law review. I immediately regretted this decision when I saw how many firms required their candidates to be on law review. But every time my law review friends told me they couldn't do anything on weekends because they had a bunch of extracurricular work to do, I was again satisfied with my decision.

Those who don't make the cut for law review count their losses and go for moot court. It's less prestigious than law review, but it's probably more fun. You get to play lawyer and argue in front of pretend judges. It's also good experience under your belt if you want to eventually become a litigator.

If your legal writing skills aren't good enough for law review and your public speaking skills aren't good enough for moot court, then you might reconsider your decision to become an attorney. Just kidding; you don't have to be in law review or moot court to succeed. It is the traditional route for top law students. But if those things don't interest you, then you shouldn't do them. Don't live your life for your résumé. Live your life first, and then worry about what employers will think. There are plenty of things you can do within law school, or outside it, that will give you a boost as a job candidate. Don't get stuck doing things you don't like just because your classmates are doing them.

No matter what activities you're involved in, or how good your résumé is, it is imperative that you prepare for on-campus interviews ahead of time. As I mentioned, OCIs sneak up on you right as you commence your second year, so it's important that you think ahead and be prepared. This might be hard to do if you're just getting settled after a long summer, but you have no choice.

After having a great time in South America, I irresponsibly milked my summer to the very last day. At the end of my first year, the day after my last exam, I packed all my earthly belongings into my car and parked it in a storage facility. I then asked a friend to drive me to the airport, and I flew to Argentina. I returned to California the day before my second-year classes started, without even having a place to live. Some good friends of mine were kind enough to let me crash on their couch while I hunted for an apartment. So I spent the first two weeks of that semester looking for an apartment, moving in, and getting settled.

I had barely bought the books for my new classes, when a friend of mine asked me, "So how many firms are you applying to?" I thought this to be a premature question, like he was asking me what I was going to have for dinner in a few months. Confused, I responded, *"Uhm,* I haven't really thought about that yet." Showing concern, he warned me, "Well you should hurry. The deadline is Wednesday." It was Monday and I had no idea what he was talking about. "The deadline for *what?"*

He looked at me like I was an idiot. The last time I had gotten a look like that was as a senior in college on September 11, 2001. I customarily rolled out of bed at around noon and did nothing for a couple of hours—not bothering to turn on a TV, or go on the internet, or talk to another human being. I did none of the things that any normal person would have done to find out that terrorists had attacked New York City and Washington, D.C., and the World Trade Center had been reduced to rubble. I wandered into my first class, late in the afternoon, whistling and smiling just as I had done on September 10th. The class was nearly empty, and the few students who had bothered to show up were huddled together talking quietly and somberly, looking devastated. It seemed like they had just heard that the professor had been murdered and there would be no class. I asked, "What's going on?" They all looked at me like I was an idiot.

"OCIs!" my friend yelled at me, four years later—almost to the exact day in September. I still looked confused.

"On-Campus Interviews," he clarified. Law students are stubborn, and never like to admit they don't know something, so I pretended I knew what he was talking about, "Oh yeah. Of course. I was just distracted."

I tracked down a classmate with whom I was closer friends, and in confidence, I asked him, "What the hell is this OCI shit people are talking about?" He too, was surprised by my ignorance, but he was more polite and explained it to me.

You should be careful not to be left out of the loop when it comes to law school matters, by the way. For some reason, the people in charge just assume that law students know everything. Law schools have been run the same way for generations, so unless there are any major changes, nobody feels the need to communicate anything to the students. You're supposed to figure everything out on your own. Nobody ever told me about OCIs. Nobody ever told me what classes I was supposed to take. Nobody ever told me I was supposed to apply for graduation. Nobody ever told me when the deadline for applying for the bar exam was, or that I was supposed to take a professional conduct exam (MPRE) during my third year. Somehow I was supposed to know all this. Supposedly, it's common knowledge.

Don't sit around and wait to be informed about something. Don't rely on administrators to let you know what's going on. Apparently they're too busy to communicate with students. Make an effort to be well-informed in advance. Talk to people, not only to professors and staff, but to students, especially the older ones who are a year or two ahead of you. Don't be afraid of looking like an idiot. Looking like an idiot, I suppose, is better than actually being one. I could always rely on my friends to keep me tuned in, but it still puzzles me how they always managed to find everything out before me. I always felt like I was the last one to know about something. It was not only irritating, but often costly.

Not finding out about OCIs until a couple of days before the application deadline caused me to be extremely unprepared, and my natural instinct was to throw my hands up in the air and give up. Fortunately, my girlfriend was in town visiting and she forced me to get my act together and apply. She helped me sort through the list of employers, finding the few that weren't out of my league. I added a few touches to my résumé and wrote a single, overly vague cover letter, changing only the name of the firm and recruiter for each application. I submitted everything electronically, barely meeting the deadline within minutes. I was in such a hurry that I didn't even have time to proofread everything. I'm sure I messed up on a few of the cover letters – addressing Tom Jones, recruiter for Smith & Barney, as Sheryl Johnson of Roberts & Patrick, and *vice versa.*

My shoddy efforts made for poor results. I didn't score a single on-campus interview. I was very upset, and thought, "All that work for nothing." But really, the work I had put toward OCIs was minimal, so I took some solace in convincing myself that if I had dedicated more time to it, I could've gotten an interview and possibly a job offer. But in all actuality, I doubt my grades were good enough.

What made me feel a little better was that it seemed as if the majority of my classmates—who were working with more than just two days notice—had also failed to land any interviews. During this time of year, you can tell who gets called for interviews by spotting the people who wear suits around campus. In case it wasn't obvious from their name, on-campus interviews are normally held on campus. And even as the working world seems to steer toward a business-casual dress code, law firms still like their job interview subjects to dress like morticians. But the main reason why law students wear their suits around campus is not to look respectable for their appointment, but to let all their classmates know that they've been chosen for an interview. Therefore, while the interview might be held in the morning and only last about 30 minutes, the student will wear the suit all day. Hell, he might wear it all week. Nothing— 100 degree heat, a pool party, a tennis match—will prompt a law student to take off his suit until *everyone* has seen him wearing it.

It is a pathetic yet common scene. Everyone will be sitting in class when a fashionably late student will walk in wearing a suit. Being overdressed for just class, everyone knows he has a job interview that day. At that moment, everyone envies him to the point of hatred. Fully aware that everyone is looking at him, he might normally feel self-conscious, but on this occasion he loves it. Today, everyone wants to be in his shoes (and matching belt), and he has never felt so important. Inevitably, someone will lean over to him and mention, "Wow. You look sharp. What's the occasion?" He'll pathetically act like he had forgotten he was so dressed up. "Oh, right," he'll play it down with feigned modesty, "I got this interview later."

On one occasion, one of my classmates—a self-proclaimed metrosexual—walked in to class wearing a ridiculously extravagant suit. His outfit was more suited for a C-list celebrity at a movie premier than for a law student at a job interview. Everyone stared at him, but not with envy. Instead, we all looked at him with a great deal of suspicion. As well as being known as the class metrosexual, he also had a reputation for being kind of dumb. Therefore, when people saw him wearing a suit, they arrived at two possible explanations: either this guy has taken this metrosexual thing *way* too far and he's wearing that suit for the sake of it, or he's wearing a suit hoping to dupe people into thinking he has an interview.

By no means was anyone willing to accept that this guy had actually landed a job interview. That would mean that he was better than most of the people in that classroom. The thought of the dumb metrosexual landing an interview made the students who had been rejected want to kill themselves. The idea that he would stoop so low as to fake an interview was much easier to stomach. The poor guy could've had the interview videotaped and broadcasted on *C-SPAN,* and people would've accused him of digitally superimposing himself.

I never did find out whether he actually had an interview. It would have been fun to surreptitiously follow him around that day and see. Either way, it goes to show you just how crazy law students get over job interviews.

Other Alternatives. On-campus interviews aren't the only way to get a summer job. But they seem to be the only way to get the really good jobs. My well-to-do friend—the one who clerked for a judge his first semester—scored a couple of on-campus interviews, and landed a coveted job with a big firm.

While he never really complained about his job, he wasn't overly enthusiastic about it either. He felt important wearing a suit to the office and working on a few cases where quite a bit of money was at stake. Since he had gone to law school straight after college, he enjoyed the fact that—all of a sudden—someone was handing him paychecks with unfathomable amounts of money on them. Checks that he could cash without ever having to worry about paying them back. Still, he cynically said that the money he made that summer didn't even cover a small fraction of the student loan debt he owed. It would take many years of a good salary for him to offset that number.

I wasn't as fortunate—or nearly as studious—as my friend, and I failed to make the cut for any on-campus interviews. Still, I kept my eyes and ears open and finally, several months after OCIs had ended, I was called for a job interview. By that point, the summer was creeping up fast, so I was pretty desperate.

I was enrolled in a Labor Law course, and the professor made an announcement about a local labor law firm that was looking for someone to work part-time during the school year and full-time during the summer. I didn't find labor law to be especially interesting, but at that point a job was a job. I submitted my résumé, along with a criminally exaggerated cover letter, emphasizing how fascinated I was by labor law, and how I wanted to dedicate the rest of my life to it.

I guess the cover letter worked, because a few days later I got called in for an interview. I hadn't been to a job interview in a pretty long time, so I was out of practice. (In fact, my last job interview had been at that bar in Sicily. It was, moreover, somewhat informal, as I was drunk and wearing sandals). I also figured this would be my last chance at a summer job, so when I arrived for the interview, I was visibly nervous. I was greeted by two women, a middle-aged partner at the firm and a young associate who had recently graduated from my law school. When they started asking me questions, I became an inarticulate idiot.

The first question—which might be one of the easiest questions ever asked at a job interview—was: "So who's your labor law professor?" I stared at them as if they had asked me to count to ten in Arabic. I blanked. For the life of me, I could not recall my professor's name. "I know this," I mumbled as I stared at the floor. I thought about it for a whole minute, managing to remember and recite aloud the name of all my other professors, but I couldn't come up with it. "I can't think of it right now," I threw my hands up in the air, admitting defeat—not only to that specific question, but to the interview in general. There was no way I was getting that job.

I struggled almost as badly with a few other easy questions. The younger woman asked, "You said in your cover letter that you've been thinking about a career in labor law. How come?" It seemed like such a standard question. In fact, I think I had even practiced an answer to it in front of the bathroom mirror. But I couldn't think of anything. *"Uhm…*well…I just…*uhm…*find it very interesting."

Trying to figure out why I wasn't nearly as passionate about labor law in real life as I had appeared in my cover letter, the older of the two women asked me, "Do you have any experience with unions?" I didn't even have to think about this one. I quickly answered, "No." But she persisted, "Do you have any family members or friends who are union members?" The only union-related experience I could think of was one time when I was eating at McDonald's, and I overheard some construction workers have a heated argument about whether they should unionize or not. At that point, the interview was such a disaster that I figured I might as well mention that experience. Anything would've been better than the silence of them waiting for my answer.

Finally, as they moved on and were about to give up on me and wish me good luck, I thought of something. *"Oh yeah,"* I yelled, nearly jumping out of my chair. I think I startled them. "I had a friend once. He was trying to be an actor and he did a few commercials. He was in S.A.G." The guy was more like a friend of a friend. I had met him one time in L.A. and he had mentioned something about the Screen Actors Guild. Even so, they weren't at all impressed. "We don't really work with those kinds of unions. Our biggest client is the local firefighter's union."

They thanked me for my interest, and I thanked them for the opportunity. On the drive home, as I played the interview back in my head, I couldn't help but to burst out in laughter. I had become an entirely different person in there. I tried to imagine what the two women might've been saying about me after I left. "Do you think he was slightly retarded?" "Probably. I mean, how do you not know your professor's name?" But the more I thought about it, the happier I was. I certainly wasn't proud of my performance, and it showed me that I desperately needed to work on my interviewing skills. But I was happy because it meant that I wouldn't be getting the job.

During the interview, they had given me a detailed description of what my responsibilities would be. It sounded like the most boring and unfulfilling job imaginable. I couldn't care less about labor law. I didn't know any union members, and there was no reason for me to feel ashamed or inadequate about that. I just wanted the job so I could tell my classmates and my parents that I had gotten a job at a law firm. I wanted the job because that's what traditional, well-to-do law students do in the summer after their second year. I convinced myself that, subconsciously, I had intentionally sabotaged the interview. My brain didn't want to come up with obvious trivia, like my professor's name, because it was afraid it would have to sit in that office for an entire summer, going over contracts for the local firefighter's union.

A couple of days later, I listened to a message left on my cell phone by the younger of the two women who had interviewed me. She politely explained, "We're sorry, but we went with someone with more union experience." Just about anyone in the world could've qualified as having more union experience than I. Initially, the sense of rejection—as it always does—made me angry. I authoritatively deleted the message and shouted at my phone, "Who did you hire, a construction worker?!" But then I smiled and breathed a sigh of relief. I didn't want to work there anyway.

That summer, I ended up working at a community law center that specialized in immigration law, a field that actually *did* interest me. It was a great experience. The law center offered free legal services to people well below the poverty line. Since they aren't paying legal fees, the clients can't really complain about having their cases handed over to inexperienced law students. Therefore, while the summer associates at big firms were doing busy work for attorneys, I had my own clients and a great deal of autonomy.

The major drawback was that I didn't get paid. The law center could barely afford to buy legal pads, much less pay its volunteer law students. But at least I got school credit for it. It would have been nice to receive a hefty paycheck and I would've loved to brag about working at a big firm, but I really *enjoyed* my time at the law center. I became very attached to my clients and got along well with my supervisors. Also, as corny as it may sound, making a difference in someone's life when they really need it *is* priceless. My clients were sincerely grateful for the work I did. I doubt I would've been able to say the same about the local firefighters union.

THIRD YEAR

For those students who get good summer associate positions and are retained by the firm to work permanently after graduation, third year of law school is pretty much a breeze. By this point, law school doesn't really have any more surprises to offer. It's just a matter of doing what you've been doing for the past two years, finishing the two semesters, and graduating.

For those who didn't get good summer jobs—or those who did, but weren't asked to come back after graduation—third year can be *very* stressful. Either way, classes are the last thing on a 3L's mind. Those with jobs lined up worry about the bar exam, while those without jobs worry about getting a job *and* the bar exam.

Early in the year, you can try your luck at another round of on-campus interviews. Though most firms recruit for summer associates, a few may be interested in hiring someone permanently. But it is more likely that you'll have to find a job elsewhere.

Government or Public Interest Work. Your law school might sponsor an alternative career fair, such as a public interest or government job fair. There's a bit of a stigma attached to this kind of work though. You will never hear a law student boasting about getting a government job. Nobody will high-five you if you become a public defender. This is due to the fact that these jobs pay considerably less money than private law firms.

Some people are capable of putting the money issue behind them and working a job for the sake of the work. They are willing to take a huge pay cut in exchange for trying to make the world a better place. I admire these people, and I'm willing to bet that while they might end up driving crappier cars, they will be happier with their work—and ultimately their lives—than their rich counterparts in the big law firms. If you're passionate about a particular field and you're not obsessed about making money, you should consider public interest work.

My supervisor at the community law center told me that when she met with her old classmates who had become phenomenally rich working at big law firms, it was *they* who actually envied *her.* Obviously, since she had dedicated her life to helping poor immigrants, her accumulation of wealth was nothing to write home about. Still, she said that the only aspect of *their* jobs that her rich former classmates liked was the money. Aside from the pride of winning a case, they couldn't care less about what happened to their clients. They weren't interested in the pursuit of justice or any higher cause; their only pursuit was a big paycheck. My supervisor was tremendously proud of her work, and every time one of her clients thanked her with a hug, it was just as good for her—if not better—as billing a client for an ungodly number of hours at an ungodly rate.

Also, she said that all the money her old classmates made came at a very high cost. They spent a majority of their lives at the office, even sleeping there on a cot when necessary. They only saw daylight on the few weekends when they didn't have to work. They all had nice houses, but what's the point of having a nice house if you don't spend any time in it? While my supervisor kept busy, she had the luxury of free time. She never had to work weekends, and she could leave the office at a reasonable hour and spend time with her children. If you could put a price on free evenings and weekends, her salary might start to resemble those of her old classmates.

The sad part is that many law students would like to do public interest work, but feel that they *can't*. Personally, I would love to dedicate my life to helping poor immigrants. But the problem is not only that law students can't resist the temptation of making a lot of money. The problem is that law students can't afford *not* to make a lot of money. Law school tuitions are so high that most law students have to borrow money and pay off the loans with interest over an extended period of time. Some students work part-time during school, but unless it's an outstanding job, it probably won't be enough to cover tuition and living expenses.

The reason that law students are so willing to pay high tuition costs and fall into debt is that they're told again and again what a good investment a law degree is. Every time I would freak out about having to take out another loan, somebody would reassure me by saying, "It's a good investment. You'll pay it off in no time." Then, after three years are up and the investment is due for a return, law students naturally want to maximize their profits. Not only to pay off the massive debt, but also to feel like they actually made a good investment. Because of this economic reasoning, law students are justifiably unwilling to take public interest jobs after graduation. It would be the equivalent to someone buying stocks on margin—borrowed money—and then donating the dividends to charity.

Maybe you're lucky enough to have wealthy and generous parents who pay for your tuition and expenses. But even then, something tells me your parents would be disappointed if after they shelled out enough money to buy a beach condo, you end up using your law degree to get convicted murderers out of death row for $25,000 a year. If your parents pay for your law school expenses, you better give them something to brag about at the country club.

As luck—or the law of supply and demand—would have it, the government jobs that nobody can afford to take are much more abundant and easier to get than the high-paying law firm jobs. But law students are stubborn; they would rather keep looking for a glamorous job than to take one that doesn't pay much.

Uncertainty. Perhaps it's this sense of exclusivity and the need to hold out for more money, but plenty of law students graduate without a job, often without any real job prospects. Leading up to graduation, it was unsettling how many of my classmates had nothing lined up. Other than the ones at the top of the class who had been offered jobs by their summer firms, as well as a few who had settled for more modest jobs at small firms or with the government, most of them were simply planning to take the bar exam and see from there. All of a sudden, after three years, the people who went to law school because they couldn't find a good job were right back where they started.

Personally, I had no idea what I was going to do. My wife and I had decided to move to Florida and I would look for a job once we got there. When people asked me what I was going to do after graduation, all I could tell them was that I was moving to Florida. At least it was something. The only thing most of my classmates could say with any certainty was, "I'm taking the bar exam in July." After that, it was a free-for-all.

What made the job search particularly difficult for me was that while I wasn't sure of many things, I was almost positive that I didn't want to be an attorney. I had been dishonest with myself in going to law school. I really wasn't that interested in a career in the law. I just figured that being a lawyer would be a well-paying job that I could handle. I forced myself through law school, bored to death by my classes and disinterested in what I was learning. The thought of forcing myself into a career as an attorney for the rest of my life was a painfully hard pill to swallow.

I started to look for non-law jobs, and I quickly learned that a law degree wasn't nearly as marketable outside the legal arena as everyone had made it out to be. Nobody cared about token graduate degrees; all they wanted was work experience. I had bypassed three years of work experience in exchange for a law degree. While I was certainly qualified for several non-law jobs, the economic issue kept rearing its head. Just as with public interest or government work, most of the entry-level non-legal jobs for which I was qualified wouldn't have paid me nearly enough to cover my student loan debt and living expenses.

I had no idea what to do. I had been in the same situation three years before when I decided to go to law school. By going to law school, all I did was put off having to make a decision, and now it was biting me in the ass. I guess I figured that three years and a new degree would change things. I was wrong. I was in the exact same situation, only now I was up to my neck in debt, married, and the father of a baby.

A few months before graduation, I talked to a friend of mine who, like so many other 3Ls, had no idea what the near future held. We commiserated with each other and agreed that law school might've been a mistake. "So what do you think you'll do?" I asked him. He stared off into space and his eyes started to light up. I could tell he had an idea, but he was hesitant to share it with me. "I don't know," he said, a little embarrassed. "This may sound stupid, but I've been thinking about maybe going to med school." I thought he was joking, so I laughed. But he didn't even smile, meaning he was actually serious. *"Med school? Are you insane?"* I could tell he re-gretted telling me his plan. "Well, I don't know. When I think about it now, I think I'd rather be a doctor than a lawyer. Deep down, I think I was always more interested in medicine than the law."

It made sense. He had an opportunity to delay having to make a decision for another four years. His father was a doctor and his older brother had a PhD, so there was a lot of pressure on him to come up with a good job. He couldn't just settle for anything. When it began to look as if he wouldn't be getting that kind of job, he probably thought another degree would do the trick. People might think he was a little crazy and overly ambitious for getting an M.D. to supplement his J.D., but nobody could consider *that* a failure. You would be hard pressed to find a set of parents disappointed in their children for obtaining a law degree *and* a medical degree. "That *bum,* Junior, is driving me crazy. He can't just be a lawyer or a doctor like everyone else's kid. He has to be *both."*

He was killing two birds with one stone: his father would be proud of him, and he wouldn't have to decide what to do for another four years. Four years is a long time; things would be different then. Surely, with a law degree *and* a medical degree, he could get any job he wanted. He was perpetuating a cycle. I envisioned my friend as a fourth-year med student, having a similar conversation with yet another classmate. "So," his classmate would ask him. "What are you doing after graduation?"

My friend would stare off into space and say, "I've been thinking about getting an M.B.A."

9

GRADUATION & ONE EXAM MORE

On graduation day, we all stood proudly, wearing our caps and gowns and congratulating each other. "We did it!" classmates shouted as they exchanged hugs and pats on the back, "I can't believe it's over."

I was happy and proud of my accomplishment. My parents flew to California to be there for the ceremony. They were proud of me, my wife was proud of me, and my daughter, had she been older than a handful of months, would likely have been proud of me too.

You would expect graduates to be cheerful on their special day, knowing that they're finally done with the long, arduous marathon. Indeed, the motivational speeches and that poignant graduation song can bring tears to the eyes of even the most reserved law student. But while graduation brings a sensation of joy and accomplishment, there is no sense of relief. As far as the graduates are concerned, the worst is yet to come.

THE BAR EXAM

Our graduation ceremony was held on a Saturday morning. The first day of the Barbri prep course, in which most of my classmates were enrolled, was scheduled for Monday morning, only two days later. The bar exam is held in July, two months after graduation. Therefore, while the graduates are happy to have their degrees, they still have a long way to go before they can relax.

If you thought studying for law school exams was bad, studying for the bar exam is about 20 times worse. You have approximately two months to learn everything you learned in law school, all over again. The exam lasts two or three days, depending on the state, and covers three years' worth of information. While, fortunately, the bar exam is not graded, it is still extremely difficult to muster a passing grade. As my graduation neared, a news story broke about how the Dean of Stanford Law School had failed the California bar exam.

Embarrassing. And if one of the nation's leading legal scholars couldn't pass, what the hell kind of a chance did *we* stand?

Almost more overwhelming than the material is the pressure. Since passing the bar exam is a prerequisite for practicing law, your law degree is practically worthless until you do. The grace period for most student loans elapses six months after graduation. That's when monthly payments begin. Therefore, most law students are impatient to pass the bar and finally start making the money they've been dreaming about for so long.

If you fail the bar exam in July, you can try again in February. Some states have a limit on how many times you can take it, while others let you take it as many times as you like, for the rest of your life. The problem is that since the exam is only offered twice a year and it takes a few months to get your test results back, a year or two can easily go by before a law grad can finally practice law and start earning any real money. Failing the bar exam in both July and February can force many to throw in the towel and consider a new career path, or at least a new jurisdiction. For example, after twice failing the notorious California bar exam, a friend of mine decided to try his luck in Nevada.

This is what is really going through the minds of the graduates as they pose for pictures and go to brunch with their relatives. It doesn't seem right. Obtaining a doctoral degree should be enough of an accomplishment on its own, but, sadly, a law degree is given little real weight until its holder passes the bar. For this reason, a law school graduation seems to have an air of premature celebration.

In an earlier chapter, I mentioned how one of my friends had somewhat arbitrarily applied to law school at the University of Iowa. That same friend came up to me on the day of graduation and told me, "Man, I wish I had gone to law school in Wisconsin." Confused, I asked him, *"Wisconsin?* What the hell are you talking about? What is it with you and these random Midwestern schools?" I couldn't imagine why a young Californian would wish to be in Wisconsin instead. I've heard of people envying celebrities and millionaires, but a law student from Wisconsin should rank pretty low on a list of people to envy. He went on to explain that students who graduate from certain accredited law schools in Wisconsin don't have to take the bar exam. The Wisconsin Bar Association thinks that a law degree is good enough. I applaud Wisconsin, and wish more states would follow its lead.

After putting it off for a while, I got around to taking the Florida bar exam in February. I'm not sure why I decided to take it, since I had made a conscious decision to not practice law for as long as I lived. Maybe it was in the name of curiosity—wanting to stare the beast in the face—or as research for this book. Maybe it was to silence all my critics—parents, relatives, in-laws, friends, former classmates, and even strangers—who couldn't comprehend why I was refusing to cash in my meal ticket and practice law. It was as if a bag full of money had fallen at my feet from the sky, and they watched in horror as I stepped over it and kept walking. Whatever my reasons for taking the bar exam, they were impure; just as my reasons for going to law school had been. And the results showed.

When I told people that I was taking the Florida bar exam, the first thing almost everyone would ask was, "Now, is Florida one of the hard ones?" Not that I have anything to compare it with, but *yes,* Florida is definitely one of the hard ones, if not one of the nearly impossible ones. As far as I'm concerned, I really don't see how any state's bar exam could be considered one of the easy ones, especially since most states have the same multi-state section (the 200 multiple-choice MBE). Lawyers in New York and California love to boast about how their exam is the hardest, and they laugh at remote states in the South or West, as if lawyers there had to pass the equivalent of a driver's license test.

My wife has a cousin who, after failing the Pennsylvania bar exam on three occasions, passed it on his fourth try. Despite his slow start, his persistence paid off: he now does perfectly well for himself as a litigator for a government office in Pittsburgh. Still, hearing his relatives, you would think he suffered from Down's Syndrome. Forget his seven years of higher education, his doctoral degree, and the fact that he's a practicing attorney; if he failed an exam on three consecutive occasions, he's an idiot. A particularly caustic uncle of his, in an insensitive attempt to reassure me as I was preparing for the test, said, "Well, you can't possibly do worse than my nephew. *Three times?* How can you fail it *three times?* And it's not like it was New York. It's *Pennsylvania.*"

Popular opinion does not do the bar exam justice. I don't care where or how many times you take it, it is never anything less than incredibly difficult. Whether it's in California or Mississippi, or whether it's your first or your fifth time, the only way to pass the bar exam is by studying like a maniac. And that's precisely where I went wrong: I studied, but not like a maniac. I studied like I had been successfully studying for exams the past three years in law school. This time around, it wasn't nearly enough.

My attitude approaching the bar exam was something like, "*Fine.* I'll take the stupid test. Are you happy now?" Needless to say, that's an incorrect and insufficient approach to tackle just about anything, especially the hardest exam on the face of the Earth. I registered late, resulting in a steep late fee, and I even missed a deadline that would have allowed me to use a laptop to type the essays. Worse yet, I was late to start studying. My wife and I were in the process of moving into a new apartment, so by the time we were settled, I had a month and a half left to study. On top of that, I had to put up with the constant distractions of the beach and the perfect climate of the Florida winter, as well as the irresistible requests of my daughter wanting to play or have a book read to her fifteen times in a row. (Now ask yourself: would you rather recite the defenses to each cause of action in torts—not so fun—or sing along with the *Cat in the Hat* as he opens the big red box for his friends Thing Two and Thing One?)

But as much as I would like to blame my shortcomings on those excuses, the truth is that my approach to studying for the exam and the way I prepared for it were what killed me. I didn't take the Barbri prep course, partly because I didn't want to—too expensive and time-consuming—but also because it was already underway when I finally started studying. Instead, I got hold of all the Barbri materials—which aren't cheap either—and followed my own routine.

I still think it's feasible to pass the bar exam without taking a prep course, though most law graduates opt to take one. Barbri has a well-regimented system with proven results, and I've heard many people say they could not have passed the exam without the help of the course. On the other hand, a friend of mine, who took a course but failed the exam, claims that it did him more harm than good. He said that attending the lectures would tire him out, and by the time he got back home, it was hard for him to study the requisite hours. He thinks he would have been better off skipping the lectures and having more time to study on his own.

More important than whether you take a course or not is how you study. As I mentioned, my study technique was the same one I had used during law school. I mostly reviewed the material, made outlines highlighting the most important points, and committed those outlines to memory. My plan was to dedicate the first month to substantive studying, and take the last few weeks to do non-stop practice testing. This had worked wonders for me in law school, so I figured that if applied in a larger scale, it would be just as suitable for the bar exam.

The problem was that I underestimated just how large a scale the bar exam is on. I began my substantive review confidently, recalling much of the information I had already learned in law school, but the material would not stop coming. It was an overwhelming amount of information—over a dozen subjects, each with millions of details—and it was supposed to all be readily available in my brain, able to come up quickly and accurately in a moment's notice. Making outlines and memorizing them was not enough. This approach had worked in law school because I was memorizing one outline for one subject at a time. Now I had 20 outlines to memorize for 20 unrelated subjects. Unless you have some sort of mutant-like photographic memory, outline review will not be enough to pass the bar exam.

Supposedly, the trick is to overdose on practice questions, not information. Starting on day one—before, after, and while you review the outlines—you have to do more practice questions than you can count. I wasted the first month trying in vain to learn and memorize everything. By the time I started with practice tests, my brain had practically exploded and I had forgotten everything.

It wasn't until a few days before the exam that it hit me like a brick. "Oh my god," I thought, "I'm going to fail the bar exam. There is no way I can pass." It may sound strange, but up to that point, the possibility of failing had never really occurred to me. Other than an occasional C, I had always done well in my law school and college exams. I could have afforded a few more points in my SATs and my LSAT, but they were enough to get me into decent schools. But this time, something was different. For the first time in my life, I walked into an exam, knowing that I would fail.

Everyone I knew annoyingly tried to boost my confidence. They told me things like, "You'll do fine. You're a smart guy." My in-laws, who are fervent born-again Christians, constantly reminded me that they were praying for me. Though well-intentioned, these encouragements were devastating. The last thing I wanted was for people to think I was dumb, or to cause them to lose faith in the power of prayer. I wished I hadn't told anyone I was taking it.

But the bar exam is too big a deal to keep a secret. If you don't think it's a big deal, all you have to do is show up for it. There's an air about it resembling the Super Bowl, or the Republican National Convention. This is especially so in Florida, where the state bar association insists on having every would-be attorney in the entire Sunshine State congregate in a single conference center. Despite having several major metropolitan areas (Miami, Tampa, Jacksonville, Orlando, etc.) spread out between hundreds of miles within a long peninsula, the Florida bar exam is held in only one location— Tampa in July and Orlando in February. A friend of mine who lives in San Francisco was mad because he had to drive about 30 minutes to Oakland to take the exam. I had to drive four hours to Orlando.

Since it was held in Orlando, my wife tagged along and took our daughter to Disney World. So while I got my ass kicked in the exam room, my two biggest supporters were riding teacups and posing for pictures with Mickey. Despite their enjoyment, having to go so far from home and being forced away from your element makes the bar exam even more stressful. You have to figure out travel arrangements, lodging, food, and several other details and expenses that needlessly complicate things. I have a hard time understanding why a state as big as Florida would choose to consolidate such a major operation into one spot, making life more difficult than it has to be, during a time that is difficult enough on its own.

Perhaps the worst part about having the bar exam in a singular location is that it is filled, packed with people. It makes a large convention center feel as congested as a subway train in Tokyo. The parking lot was a nightmare, and the lobby where the registration booths were set up resembled Chicago's O'Hare airport on the busiest travel day of the holiday season. After registering and getting my ticket, I had to wait in a long, slow-moving security line that went through a metal detector. I'm not sure if they were screening for cheating devices or weapons. I felt like a cow in a slaughterhouse, being led against my will toward a gruesome death.

The bright side of there being so many people present is that you get to meet some interesting characters. During the morning of the first day, many people were confused about where to go and what to do. One middle-aged guy was being extremely helpful, pointing people in the right direction and telling them where to go, sort of like an air-traffic controller. I figured he was a staff member doing his job, but he turned out to be a fellow exam-taker. I asked him how come he knew the system so well, and he boastfully announced, "Man, I've done this so many times, I could do it with my eyes closed." This is one occasion in which a lot of experience is nothing to brag about. This guy had taken and failed the exam so many times that he was now an expert on everything about the bar exam (except, of course, the exam itself).

That's the funny thing about taking the February bar; first-timers are a minority. From what I gathered, the majority of people seemed to be having a second go at it after failing in July. When I told the guy sitting behind me that it was my first time, he looked at me suspiciously, like I was embarrassed to tell anyone I had failed in the past. When I finally convinced him, he got this nurturing, paternal look about him and said, "A virgin huh? Well, good luck to you, buddy." He had failed at least twice before, and he appeared certain that he would fail yet again. When the last section was over, he put his pencil down, leaned back on his chair, and said, "I'll see you folks in July."

I also knew that I had failed, though I maintained a small inkling of hope until the official results arrived two months later. Maybe I had gotten lucky in my 150 or so guesses. In the end, it was the Florida multiple choice section that killed me, particularly all the impossibly detailed procedural questions about statutes and codes that would never come up in a law school exam—especially not one in California. I did well in the essays and held my own on the multi-state section, but it wasn't enough.

When I left the exam room, I felt like I had been run over by a mini-van. The kind of headache I had was worse than when I cracked my skull open snowboarding in Lake Tahoe. Comparatively, I had it pretty easy; my friends in California had a whole third day to endure. I think a convincing argument could be made before the United Nations that the bar exam qualifies as state-sponsored torture. My wife took me to Disney World to celebrate, though I assure you it wasn't my top choice. I was afraid I would bring the mood down and ruin the theme park for all the tourists. All I wanted was beer, aspirin, and my bed—a four-hour drive away.

CONCLUSION

During the graduation commencement ceremony they don't give you your actual diploma. They symbolically hand you something that resembles a diploma from a distance. It's an elegant folder in which to put your diploma when you actually get it a few months later, after they check to see if you passed all your classes for the last semester. Supposing they had given me my actual diploma, and for some reason, someone offered to buy it back from me for a full refund of the tuition, I would've taken the money. Hell, at that point I was so broke I probably would've sold it for half-price.

There's a man who appears regularly on television selling vacuum cleaners. He has a generous guarantee where he allows you to order a vacuum cleaner and try it out, and if you don't like it, he gives you your money back and even covers the shipping costs. I wish law schools had a similar policy. I suspect that many disappointed law students would ask for their money back. But law schools don't have a money back guarantee, so before you make such a major commitment, you should be well aware of what you're getting into, and evaluate your reasons for wanting to attend.

I thought back to my reasons for going to law school. The main reason was that I didn't know what else to do. After three years and about $100,000 later, I *still* had no idea. I had just managed to postpone the inevitable.

Another reason was that part of me wanted to obtain an advanced professional degree. Now that I think about it, this was mostly to please my parents and family, who had high expectations for me. When I graduated from college, my grandfather called to congratulate me and asked me, "So when are you going to go back to school and get a *real* degree?" After graduating from law school, he congratulated me and immediately asked, "So when are you going to start working?" There's no pleasing some people, so it's better to not even try. Since you're the one who has to live your life, it's much more important to consider *your* strengths, goals, and dreams.

I also thought that if I went to law school I could make a lot of money. As I wore my cap and gown and received my pretend diploma, the only money to my name was six figures worth of student-loan debt. On top of that, there were no foreseeable paychecks in my immediate future. I was confident that the paychecks would eventually come, but it didn't seem they would be as high as I had fantasized them to be.

Finally, I figured a law degree would be a valuable and marketable degree. Now, I realize that a J.D. is perfectly marketable, but only if you want to work as an attorney. Otherwise, it's just an added bonus on your résumé. It may impress some employers, but not necessarily more than speaking Chinese or being good with computers.

Don't get me wrong. Retrospectively, I don't think going to law school was the right decision for me. But that doesn't mean it was a complete waste of my time. I met some interesting people and made some very good friends. I got to live in California and thoroughly enjoy myself when school didn't interfere. Perhaps most importantly, I underwent a rigorous academic marathon comparable to Marine Corp boot camp, reading court cases instead of doing push-ups. After completing law school, all other intellectual endeavors will seem like a friendly game of bingo.

I also learned a few valuable things about the law. For example, in my Evidence class, I learned that if you tell someone that you're sorry after causing any sort of accident, your apology can be used against you in court as an admission of guilt. One day, as I was driving on the Santa Monica Freeway in Los Angeles, I rear-ended a car in front of me. Though there was no major damage to the car, a distraught girl got out and, on the verge of tears, she hysterically sulked, *"God,* I can't believe this. I just got my car out of the shop because someone rear-ended me two weeks ago." The poor girl just wanted some sympathy from me, but the law student inside my head kept telling me, "Don't apologize. It's an admission of guilt. Whatever you do, do *not* apologize."

The only thing that I could think to say other than sorry was, "Are you alright?" "Yes, I'm fine," she protested, "It's just that now I have to go through all this insurance crap again. And I'll have to take my car back to the shop." She looked at me expecting an apology. Any other normal person in the world would've said sorry, but I wouldn't allow myself. "The important thing is that you're alright," I said as I gave her my insurance information. She gave me a dirty look, walked back to her car, and drove off. I felt terrible for not apologizing. Once she was gone, I covered my mouth with my hand, and muttered under my breath, "I'm sorry."

I guess it's good to know things like that. Then again, had I just apologized and been nicer to the girl, perhaps she might have not even bothered to bring the insurance companies into it. My non-apology may not have incriminated me, but sorry or not, it was pretty obvious that the accident had been my fault. After all, I had slammed into the back of her motionless car.

Aside from anything I might've learned, the only real and tangible thing that my law degree has given me is the right to practice law within the United States. Of course, a few more hurdles have to be jumped, the biggest of which is obviously the bar exam. After all is said and done, that's what law school is. It's a hurdle that has to be jumped on the way to becoming a lawyer. My problem is that I never really wanted to be an attorney. Now, after graduating, I felt forced to become one.

When I was in my third year, my younger brother, a senior in college, was facing an almost identical dilemma to the one I had faced at his age. He told me, "I'm thinking about going to law school." I asked him, "Are you absolutely positive that you want to be a lawyer and work as an attorney?" He thought about it for a second and said, "Not really." Bluntly, I told him, "Then don't go to law school."

As the number of applicants to law school grows annually, I can't help but wonder how many of these applicants are truly going to law school for the right reasons. In those statistics, I see people like my brother, like myself, and like my many disillusioned classmates. To them, I give the same advice I gave to my brother: unless you're *sure* that you want to be a lawyer, don't go to law school.

That's the primary reason why I wrote this book. I felt that I had made a mistake in going to law school and I wanted to help people in a similar situation from doing the same thing. Also, since I have no real intentions of practicing law in the near future, I wanted something tangible to show for my efforts as a law student. I figured that after three years and thousands of dollars, I should at least have something to write about. And who knows? I might even sell a few copies and pay off some of my student loans.

Epilogue

After graduation, I bounced around for a while. First came the move: a brutal drive across the United States, from California to Florida. I had a hyper-ambitious vision of an All-American road trip—stopping at national parks, monuments, and general places of interest along the way—but one of my wife's friends had annoyingly scheduled her wedding on a date that gave us no time for leisure. We sped through major highways, took no touristy detours, and the only things we stopped to see were gas stations and roadside motels.

The worst part of having to cut our trip short and get to Florida in a rush was that I planned to start my job hunt as soon as I arrived, and this was something that I was not in a hurry to do. Not that I didn't want to start working—I desperately wanted the comfort and security of full-time employment—I just didn't want to go through the process of searching and obtaining a job. I wished I could just close my eyes and wake up six months later, having found work, being past the awkward first few weeks or months of a job—when you have no idea what you're doing, and you keep meeting people but immediately forgetting their names—and being settled down with a nice steady routine. (Since we are wishing for things, why not add a smart long-term financial plan, a house, and, while we're at it, the ability to fly). But life, even when it is less than pleasant, has to be lived in its entirety. I could not avoid the working world any longer.

First, my father-in-law approached me and suggested I join the family business. I had always fantasized about the idea of nepotism, though it had never before been an option for me. Since my father is a doctor, the only job he could've ever helped me get required even more schooling than I'd just gone through. Now, having married into a profitable family-owned corporation, I finally had my chance. But it didn't prove to be nearly as glamorous as I had envisioned it. I had to share an office with my sister-in-law, and I couldn't even talk bad about my boss at home since he inconveniently happened to be my wife's dad. I helped out for a few months, and moved on.

At this point, I took two months to study and take the bar exam. (We all know how well *that* turned out). Then, while I awaited the test results and searched for a permanent job, I signed up for temp work with a legal consulting firm. To call it a legal consulting firm is generous; it was essentially a sweat shop for recent law grads and out-of-work attorneys. Whenever major firms encounter too much of a workload for their own staff to handle, they commonly out-source some of the grunt work to consulting firms or legal services firms such as this one. It baffles me that they wouldn't just send the work to India and save a fortune. If Thomas Friedman has taught us anything, it's that there's not much future for such jobs in the United States.

The work consisted of reviewing thousands upon thousands of documents (mostly emails), and tagging any which might be used as evidence in a pending case. For every 500 documents I read, only one or two would turn out to be remotely relevant. The other 498 were junk mail—cookie recipes, offers to purchase Viagra, you name it. I was called to work on a big, expensive case, involving a major bank. The bank, of course, hired one of those snooty large firms that only recruits associates from Harvard. Since those attorneys are being paid too much to read irrelevant emails, they turned the tedious task over to me and about fifty other down-on-their-luck law grads.

The lead attorney trying the case flew in from her San Francisco office to administer a training session. Before she arrived, our supervisor urged us to "Try to appear smart, like you know what you're doing. Don't ask too many stupid questions." That wasn't a sufficient deterrent, however, as many stupid questions were asked. There were some dumb lawyers in that room. Everyone was in awe of the lead attorney. She was a petite, surprisingly young woman, but even though she was perfectly nice and down-to-earth, everyone was intimidated by and jealous of her. They all wanted her life—the life they had in mind when they had decided to go to law school. Some approached her in conversation, with delusional hopes that she might take them back to San Francisco with her, like some sort of rags-to-riches story. Today: sifting through some secretary's junk-mail folder in a glorified call center. Tomorrow: partner at an elite 500-lawyer firm.

While most of the temps were licensed attorneys, the firm would also take recent law grads who were actively pursuing admittance into the Bar. However, the second requirement was rather lax, since there were several temps who had long ago graduated from law school and were still not members of the Bar. One, who actually had risen to the level of pod-supervisor—responsible for reviewing the work of about 25 temps—had a law degree, and had successfully passed the Bar Exam, but could not pass the Florida Bar Association's strict character test. He had gotten into some trouble in his past—normal, rebellious-youth misconduct—and it was now keeping him from practicing law. Another woman, from what I was able to gather, had no background in the law whatsoever. She was a talker, and told all kinds of exaggerated stories about her past, though none even remotely related to the study, practice, or existence of law. And then, of course, there were several Bar Exam failures, gearing up to take it (and quite possibly fail it) again.

Though there was not much of a differentiation between the licensed and non-licensed temps—everyone was given the same duties and pay—a certain *de facto* caste system was ever-present. There was one instance when a case came in, and the outsourcing firm requested that all document reviewers be licensed attorneys. A sign-up sheet for the case was passed around the pod, with two bits of information required: name and Bar number. It felt to some like living during segregation or Apartheid; all the non-licensed law grads could only hang their heads and accept the fact that there were certain things they could not do. The actual attorneys would beam with pride, and make a big deal about that coveted Bar number: "Damn. I've forgotten my Bar number again. I don't know how I can't remember it. It's like forgetting your phone number. Oh wait, *here* it is. It's tattooed on my forearm."

But in all honesty, though the licensed attorneys had bragging rights and access to some off-limit cases, they were in no position to boast. This was nobody's top choice for employment. Everyone was looking for something more permanent and stable. There were a few solo practitioners who used the gig for supplemental income and benefits, but most of the temps were out-of-work attorneys looking for a full-time job.

The case lasted about six weeks until we started to run out of documents. Word spread that we were down to the last few hundred emails to review, and soon we would be told to go home. "Everybody work as *slow* as you can," one of the more desperate temps suggested, "I need this to last me through the week." Even the pod-supervisor, though he couldn't advise us to work slowly, had a gloomy look about him. Once the documents for this case were depleted, we would be sent home, and there was no knowing when the next case would come in. Nobody knew when they might work again.

I was sad that my appointment at the consulting firm was over. I had enjoyed my time there, and I had grown quite attached to some of my pod-mates. Every afternoon, when the work got too dull and repetitive, we would have long, unproductive conversations about sports, the tabloids, and old action movies (there was an unusual obsession among the male temps with the early films of Schwarzenegger and Stallone). Usually on Fridays, our pod-supervisor, the one whose criminal past had kept him from admission into the Bar, would regale us with old tales of drugs and vandalism. Though he clearly regretted not being able to practice law, judging from the enthusiasm with which he told his stories, he wouldn't have traded his past for even a seat in the Supreme Court.

Fortunately for me, just as the case was winding down, I was called in for an interview and offered a permanent job, where I would begin work as an administrative director with a university. Therefore, unlike all the other temps, I was in the enviable position of not worrying about being left without a job. Sometime later I received the bad news about the bar exam, so I took it as a blessing for the path I was following outside the legal arena.

Part of the reason why I had gone to law school was that I have always felt drawn to the environment of academia. If there is one thing American society has gotten right, it is its universities. There is nothing quite like a leafy campus, closed off from the rest of the world, with students strolling unhurried or breezing by on bicycles, and empty beer cans scattered around still to be picked up from the night before, offering a constant reminder that life—at least for a brief few years—can and should be care-free and enjoyable. Believe it or not, law schools exist harmoniously within these leafy college campuses. (Unfortunately, though, many law schools choose to set up in downtown areas, away from the undergraduate campus and closer to such amenities as law firms and courthouses.)

Perhaps it's a case of arrested development, of refusing to grow up, but I wanted to stay within the university environment. Some of my law school friends, who had similar attachments to the student life, stayed on for more schooling. One decided to stay another year and do the JD/MBA, while another went for an LLM. My crazy friend who decided to go to medical school after graduation actually went back to college as an undergrad, to take the required pre-med courses he needed. As much as I would have loved to, I could no longer be a student. I needed to work to support my wife and daughter. So I figured the next best thing would be to get a job with a university.

Also, higher education is perhaps the only industry where token graduate and professional degrees actually count for something. As I applied for the job, one of the qualifications required was "Master's Degree or higher." It didn't even specify a discipline, only that the candidate have a graduate degree. I could have just as easily had a PhD in Extraterrestrial Studies. I had finally found a job outside the legal arena where my JD was actually worth something.

The job has suited me quite well. In researching and writing this book, I developed an interest for university administration. There were certain policies and procedures in law school that made little sense to me, and I wondered who, if anyone, was responsible for them. Now *I* am the one responsible for many of those same academic policies and procedures.

But although I am satisfied with my job and my life, I don't know how much longer I can escape the law. I don't mean that I am a fugitive evading law enforcement officials. I mean that not a day goes by where I don't think about what my life would be like if I had just followed the traditional law-student route. Whenever I talk to my old classmates, or other attorneys, and they talk about law firm life, I feel a little emptiness inside, like I am missing out on an experience that was meant for me. After all, I did enjoy my time working with indigent clients at the immigration law center, and there are many other immigrants who have money and who do need help. I could see myself helping them, and taking pro bono cases for those who couldn't afford it, in a firm or solo practice that would actually have meaning and reward both to them and to me.

I also sometimes feel that I am selling myself short, and that with the level of education I have attained, I should be doing bigger things. Whenever a task is assigned to me at work that is the least bit menial, I get this uppity air—just for a moment—when I ask myself if it isn't beneath me: "I have a *law degree*. I should be out there suing people. What the Hell am I doing *here?*"

*　　*　　*

I didn't think I want to be a lawyer, and I don't think I ever really did. But at this point, after having come this far, being a lawyer is something I think I need to do. Perhaps the study of law just gets in our blood, and leaves behind a growing sense of commitment to the law itself. After the bar exam, I thought about selling my Barbri books on eBay, and never thinking about the law again. But I couldn't. I kept them, and will sit for the Florida Bar Exam again in the near future. Though it will not be any easier, I am confident that I will pass the second time around.

As for a career, my top choice would be for this book to sell like hot cakes, and live off the royalties…in Hawaii. But if that doesn't happen—or until that day—I might well be on a gradual and semi-reluctant transition into becoming an attorney. It could take a year or a lifetime, but I would bet that at some point it will happen, and when it does, I'm not sure it will be such a terrible thing after all. I'll see you in court.

ABOUT THE AUTHOR

Juan Doria has a B.A. in English from Indiana University–Bloomington, and a J.D. from a competitive law school in California. He currently lives in Florida with his wife and daughter. This is his first book.

INDEX

T

U

W

Y

OTHER BOOKS

Grains of Golden Sand: Adventures in War-Torn Africa,
by Delfi Messinger
Hardcover 978-1-888960-35-8,
391 pages, US$21.95
Softcover 1-888960-33-4,
391 pages, US$15.95

Grab a ticket for the adventure of a
lifetime: meet a woman who protects
rare apes by painting, in blood, SIDA
("AIDS" in French) on a Kinshasa
wall to keep rampaging looters at bay.

Her mission was to save a small group of endangered great apes—the
"bonobo" (or "sexy" ape)—from the grip of civil war in the heart of
Zaire. She made this her mission, and after eight harrowing years the
reader will be breathless with amazement in her struggles to get the
endangered animals to safety.

Training Wheels for Student Leaders: A Junior Counseling
Program in Action, by Autumn Messinger
ISBN 978-1-888960-13-6, US$21.95

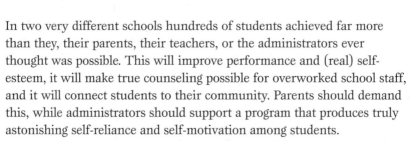

A reference for the engaged parent,
founded on the premise that, if given the
opportunity, mentoring, and guidance,
even young children can work together
to solve (and resolve) their own
problems. They can work towards their
own, common, cooperative goals. They
can build genuine self-esteem.

In two very different schools hundreds of students achieved far more
than they, their parents, their teachers, or the administrators ever
thought was possible. This will improve performance and (real) self-
esteem, it will make true counseling possible for overworked school staff,
and it will connect students to their community. Parents should demand
this, while administrators should support a program that produces truly
astonishing self-reliance and self-motivation among students.

FOR THE LAW STUDENT

LAW SCHOOL: GETTING IN, GETTING GOOD, GETTING THE GOLD,
by Thane Messinger
ISBN: 978-1-888960-80-8, 224 pages, US$16.95

Finally a book for *real* law students—not preachy
and not unrealistic. This book focuses on skills that
are readily fine-tuned, with practical advice that is
workable with today's ultra-busy lifestyle. The key
in successful law study is a minimum of wasted effort and a maximum
of results. Still outlining cases? A waste of time. Failing to use
hypotheticals? A dangerous omission. Preparing a huge outline? A
dangerous waste of time. Don't waste your time, and don't neglect what's
truly important. Learn law school techniques that work. Once you're in,
Get Good, and Get the Gold!

LATER-IN-LIFE LAWYERS: TIPS FOR THE NON-TRADITIONAL LAW
STUDENT, by Charles Cooper
ISBN 978-1-888960-06-8, 288 pages, US$18.95

Law school is a scary place for any new student.
For an older ("non-traditional") student, it can be
intimidating as well as ill-designed for the needs of
a student with children, mortgages, and the like.
Includes advice on families and children; the LSAT, GPAs, application
process, and law school rankings for non-traditional students; paying for
law school; surviving first year; non-academic hurdles; and the occasional skeleton in the non-traditional closet.

PLANET LAW SCHOOL II: WHAT YOU NEED TO KNOW (BEFORE YOU
GO)—BUT DIDN'T KNOW TO ASK…AND NO ONE
ELSE WILL TELL YOU, by Atticus Falcon
ISBN 978-1-888960-50-7, 858 pages, US$24.95

An encyclopedic reference for each year of law
school. Examines hundreds of sources, and offers
in-depth advice on law courses, materials, methods,
study guides, professors, attitude, examsmanship, law review, internships, research assistantships, clubs, clinics, law jobs, dual degrees,
advanced law degrees, MBE, MPRE, bar review options, and the bar
exam. Sets out all that a law student must master to excel in law school.

FOR THE NEW ATTORNEY

JAGGED ROCKS OF WISDOM: PROFESSIONAL ADVICE FOR THE NEW
ATTORNEY, by Morten Lund
ISBN: 978-1-888960-07-5, US$18.95

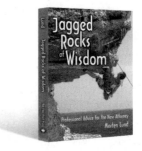

Written by a real-world mentor at a
national law firm, this no-nonsense guide
is a must-have guide for the new associate. Its "21 Rules of Law Office Life" will
help make the difference to your success
in the law: surviving your first years as
an attorney, and making partner. Beware.
Avoid the dangers. Read, read, and read
again these 21 Rules of Law Office Life.

THE YOUNG LAWYER'S JUNGLE BOOK: A SURVIVAL GUIDE,
by Thane Messinger
ISBN 978-1-888960-19-1,
231 pages, US$18.95

A career guide for summer associates,
judicial clerks, and all new attorneys.
Now in its 12th year and second edition,
hundreds of sections with advice on law
office life, advice on law office life,
including working with senior attorneys,
legal research and writing, memos,
contract drafting, mistakes, grammar, email, managing workload,
timesheets, annual reviews, teamwork, department, attitude, perspective,
working with clients (and dissatisfied clients), working with office staff,
using office tools, and yes, much more.